GLOBAL THEC

THE UNIVERSITY COLLEGE OF
RIPON AND YORK ST. JOHN

Rex Ambler

GLOBAL
THEOLOGY

*The meaning of faith in the
present world crisis*

SCM PRESS
London

TRINITY PRESS INTERNATIONAL
Philadelphia

First published 1990

SCM Press
26–30 Tottenham Road
London N1 4BZ

Trinity Press International
3725 Chestnut Street
Philadelphia, Pa. 19104

© Rex Ambler 1990

British Library Cataloguing in Publication Data

Ambler, Rex
Global theology.
1. Theology
I. Title
230

ISBN 0–334–02434–X

Library of Congress Cataloging-in-Publication Data

Ambler, R. A.
Global theology / Rex Ambler.
p.   cm.
ISBN 0–334–02434–X
1. Human ecology—Religious aspects—Christianity.
2. Christianity and international affairs. 3. Economics—Religious
aspects—Christianity. 4. World politics—1985–1995. 5. East and
West. 6. North and South. 7. Christianity and culture. I. Title.
BT695.5.A46 1990   89–71080
261.8—dc20

169659

Photoset by J&L Composition Ltd, Filey, North Yorkshire
and printed in Great Britain by
Richard Clay Ltd, Bungay, Suffolk

CONTENTS

If way to the Better there be,
it exacts a full look at the Worst

Thomas Hardy
In Tenebris II

*

I am grateful to my students at the university who have taken up these issues so enthusiastically and enabled me to clarify them in preparing the book. I would also like to thank some individuals who have read all or part of an earlier draft of the book and offered friendly and/or expert advice. Jorge Larrain, a sociologist of world development, and Andrew Nickson, a global economist, have both advised me on chapter 2. Nick Lampert, a specialist on Soviet affairs and East/West relations, helped on chapter 3. Jonathon Porritt of Friends of the Earth helped on the ecological questions of chapter 4. Angela Hippisley-Cox and Stephen Pattison gave me much encouragement in the early stages. Judy Tweddle proof-read the final draft. I hope they all like the result.

ONE

Introduction

The globe is too vast and complex for any of us to understand, and yet each of us needs to have some idea of it, if it is only the vaguest image. Indeed a vague, impressionistic image is probably all that any of us can get, both because of the complexity of the globe and because of our own involvement in it. Yet some images are better than others. The appropriate question for us to ask is what sort of image is most adequate to the reality of the globe as it impinges on our everyday life.

Global worries

That question is now more serious and urgent than ever. It is part of the awareness of most thoughtful people in the modern world that the globe is in some sense in crisis, and that the crisis affects them, or might affect them, personally. They are aware, for example, both that the security interests of America and Russia are under threat *and* that as a result the security of the rest of us is under threat. They are aware too that generating and distributing wealth is now part of a global system, that that system is unstable and unfair, and that consequently our own economic security is weakened. And most people are now becoming aware of a global ecological crisis which is in some way linked with our over-enthusiastic industrial enterprise. The recent accident at Chernobyl made many people aware for the first time of the global dimensions of our ecological problems, for here the destructive power that was unleashed was beyond human control and could reach beyond the boundaries of nations and power blocs. If it is not clear how these issues are linked – this is a matter I want to discuss – it is at least clear that each separately is linked to our own fate, whoever we happen to be and wherever we happen to live on the globe.

At another level, and again without being aware necessarily of the link with the larger global issues, people are conscious of a global connection in many of the local issues which trouble them. Mass unemployment, for example, is a worrying enough issue in itself. It would perhaps be psychologically manageable if we could believe that new initiatives from government or capital could eventually get rid of it. But we know this is not the case. We know that, despite the rhetoric of our major political parties, unemployment cannot be overcome at the national level because it is not so much an internal management problem as an international economic problem. *Our* unemployment is part of, and only intelligible in terms of, world unemployment. This daunting discovery can sap any energy we might have to do something about the situation, unless we can also discover from the global connection a dynamic of hopeful change.

There is a similar feeling about our inner cities, racial tensions and the increase in crime. As soon as we ask why the inner cities are so desolate, why black and Asian people in these areas or elsewhere in Britain are so poorly treated, or why young people are so deeply frustrated, we have to look beyond the cities themselves and beyond our national boundaries to the big 'global city' in which all of us now live.

This awareness can lead to a very dark view of the prospect for humankind, since it can then appear that our fate is determined by forces too large and powerful for any of us to change. It can also be a spur to new idealism, as we are witnessing in the remarkable response of Live Aid and Sport Aid to the famine in Africa, in which the global media, normally devoted to narrow self-interest, have been made to serve a genuinely global sense of compassion. It is significant too that against the trend of jingoistic government propaganda we should be concerned en masse about suffering in a remote part of the globe. Doesn't this in itself betoken a new kind of global awareness, perhaps a sense of global identity?

2

This is not to say that donations of money to areas of need make up an adequate response to the crisis concerned. In point of fact they rather show up the profound *in*adequacy of our institutions to deal with crises of a global dimension. They show what nations *could* do, for example through the United Nations, if they weren't so pig-headedly preoccupied with their national self-interest. And they expose the futility and shortsightedness of this kind of nationalism in a world that has become interdependent. But even with these insights we would not have touched the nerve of the problem, for we have not even begun to ask *why* Africa is so poor or *why* the superpowers have been at loggerheads, or whether perhaps there is any connection between the two.

There is obviously a general reluctance to ask questions of this sort, and to be honest I am not quite sure how to account for it. My suspicion is that in this line of thought one worry leads to another. And along the line I can see two big worries in particular. The first is that our problems then become so big that we cannot think of doing anything to affect them significantly, so that we feel helpless and powerless. The second is that if we look too hard for the people who are chiefly responsible for the world's ills we might find too many fingers pointing back at us. There are certainly many analysts and political leaders in the South who confidently hold the North responsible for their poverty, as there are ideologues in the East who will blame the West for the costly and dangerous arms race. Perhaps we should face up to these charges and take their analyses more seriously than we do. But the fact is we should not change very much by simply taking the blame, for by itself this merely induces guilt which is not very productive. If we are to respond constructively to problems of a global scale we need to understand them well enough to know what broad social changes would make a difference and how individually we can do the *right* thing to promote these changes rather than blindly continue to do the wrong thing.

Western expansion

As a first step in this direction it would seem that we in the West have to recognize that the global problems that most worry us are closely connected with the spread of our own Western civilization. This is not to say that they are caused by it alone – there is after all the alarming rate of increase in the world's population which has only little to do with Western intervention. But it can be said, as I will argue more in detail later, that the greatest single factor in bringing our world problems to a critical state is the present domination of modern Western culture. That is indeed a strong claim to make, but before trying to back it up let me say something about what it means. In speaking of the 'domination' of the West I have two distinct developments in mind. First, Western countries have over the centuries acquired political and economic dominance in the world, although the centre of power has shifted over time from Europe to North America, and the mode of domination has changed from imperial control to economic pre-eminence and manipulation. (From one point of view Russia may be said to share this domination, as an originally European civilization that expanded into Asia.) Secondly – and here the development is more complex – the distinctive culture of the modern West, the culture of modernity, has now become the dominant culture of most countries in the world. This is what J. M. Roberts called 'the triumph of the West' (in his persuasive television series of that name, now published as a book).[1] It is not the conquest of one country by another, but the spread of a culture and a way of life, which also, as it happens, tends to reinforce economic and political dependencies. The process, however, is gradual. The point of entry for Western culture has usually been our technology, which is that aspect of our culture least likely to conflict with the indigenous culture and most likely to show immediate benefits. But once having a foot in the door it is better able to introduce other features of modernity which seem to be necessary to sustain technological advance. Arnold Toynbee summarizes the process rather sceptically: the victim

> gives a grudging admission to the most trivial, and therefore least upsetting, of these poisonous splinters of a foreign way of life, in the hope of being able to get off with no further concessions than just that; and then, as one thing leads to another, he finds himself compelled to admit

the rest of the intruding culture piecemeal. No wonder that the victim's normal attitude towards an intrusive alien culture is a self-defeating attitude of opposition and hostility.[2]

In this way more and more countries have taken over Western-style education, democratic government (at least in name, which is significant in itself), rationalization in business and industry, modern science and the scientific outlook, television entertainment, ideals of personal ambition and social mobility, and much much more. At a deeper level they have imbibed the Western belief in fundamentally improving the quality of life by increasing the quantity of goods through industrial production and technological innovation.

Despite the success of this global invasion we have somehow to come to terms with the fact that the culture is now being called in question by its own historical achievement. Even if we wish to maintain that it worked in the past when only the West was modernized – perhaps because it could depend on vast resources in the 'undeveloped', i.e. unmodernized, world – we would have to admit that it cannot be said to be working now for the world as a whole. The reasons for this we shall have to look into, but I think it is worth reflecting on the thought that in the nature of the case Western culture is bound to have a limited life and the likelihood is that its term is now due. If we consider what it is that has given the West its remarkable dynamic, producing the materially most powerful culture that has ever existed, we would have to single out a trend which began with the exploration of the globe in the fifteenth century (perhaps earlier with the Crusades), moved on to the scientific exploration of the heavens, the economic adventures of early capitalism and the extraordinary mechanical innovations of the industrial revolution, and then peaked with the European empires of the last century which more or less covered the globe. One mode of expansion followed another, building on the success of the one before. In retrospect we can view this history as one historical movement, as one massive project of expansion and control, although few of the people involved may have perceived it as such. Francis Bacon was one of the few who did: in *The Advancement of Learning* (1605), he

5

recommended the planned development of science as an attempt to 'gain for the mind the authority which properly belongs to it', and to exercise that authority by exploiting the earth 'for the benefit and use of man, for the relief of man's estate'. The project presupposed a new world view – made possible no doubt by the Reformation view of the transcendence of God, but not a necessary consequence of it[3] – that the whole earth is created for the benefit of humankind and that it can and should be thoroughly exploited to that end; that the greatest benefit the earth can yield is material enrichment; that the appropriate way to acquire this is to gain complete mastery through knowledge and manipulation (the political model of power); that the appropriate knowledge is detached, impersonal, abstract, analytical and reductionist (reducing all processes to material ones, thereby giving priority to physics).[4] These assumptions, whether held consciously or not, were probably necessary to the daring historical project that followed in the next few centuries. They also became part of the whole outlook of Western culture as more and more of life, natural and human, came under its sway.

Johan Galtung uses these philosophical ideas to describe what he calls the 'social cosmology' or 'deep ideology' of Western society. In answer to the question 'What is the real nature of the Western enterprise?' he suggests 'the idea emerges that expansion from a centre in the Inner-West represents progress',[5] that 'In Western cosmology space, time and knowledge combine into expansionism based on a few crucial dimensions',[6] and, hinting at the inevitable crisis involved, a combination of 'on the one hand insatiable expansionism, with no built-in stop signal, and on the other hand exploitative, vertical relations to human beings and to nature, seen as normal/natural and as instruments for expansion to take place'.[7]

The inevitable crisis is that in a limited world there must be a limit to expansion. When the expansion is primarily material, as in the Western enterprise, the limits are starkly obvious, since, to state the obvious, the globe is of a certain size. (Do the present ventures into space represent futile gestures of defiance at these limits of size?) When the expansion is exploitative, whether innocently or cynically –

drawing its power from others – it will meet its limits in the form of depleted resources. Further, when the mode of exploitation is predominantly mechanical manipulation it will sooner or later undermine the very (non-mechanical) processes of life on which it depends.

It should not therefore be too surprising when e.g. the delicate life-systems around the deserts give way to desertification, or when life in the ever-expanding cities becomes unbearable, or when wars become too dangerous to fight. But it nevertheless comes as a shock for those of us who have believed in this expansionist project – and who in the modern world has not believed in it? – to come up against its limits in hard reality. When so much of our life in the West is bound up with the hope of an ever-increasing expansion, how can we envisage life without it, except gloomily as a return to the Dark Ages? How can we believe in our hearts rather than merely in our heads that the civilization that has given us modern science, democracy, individual rights and freedoms, and unparalleled wealth and leisure should be too unstable to last – and more than that, that it should be responsible for its own eventual downfall? Perhaps this is hardest for those who are still basking in the achievements of the West; for the rest, according to their proximity to privilege, it is not so difficult.

Global theology

In either case what begins as a material crisis in the depletion of resources or the threat of nuclear war becomes eventually a spiritual crisis. This may first become apparent when we discover again, in a new form, an age-old truth about the insecurity of this world. The most impressive material securities that our drive and technology have been able to construct will appear fragile in the face of a crisis on this scale. We begin to wonder where our security lies. We then discover that the material threats posed are directly or indirectly the result of our pursuit of material security. This paradox questions some of the deepest assumptions on which our lives are based. It forces us to ask questions for which no answer can be found in modern science or in the practical wisdom of our future-oriented age: e.g.

How do we as human beings, and I as an individual, fit into the general scheme of things?

What am I, what are we, if we are not mechanical objects describable wholly by physics?

What makes for a full human life, if it is not the acquisition of material things?

What can we trust in life beyond the power to defeat or outdo others?

What is the ultimate basis of our security and our identity?

What meaning or value is there beyond the purposes of personal ambition and social progress?

How can we survive?

Questions like these are notoriously difficult to answer. Most of us shy away even from articulating the questions themselves. But if we do ask them it is likely that we should find fitting answers only through a process of self-discovery, for we should have to struggle, among other things, with the false and yet comfortable self-images which are themselves a form of man-made security. But it is also valuable, and I think necessary, to share this search with others in the hope of helping one another along the way. In many respects, for all the intimacy and privacy of genuine self-discovery, we share a common human situation, and now especially we share a common global worry. Unless we can come together across long-established boundaries of religion and ideology we have little hope of resolving our common crises. We must find a discourse in which we can communicate both our global concerns and our spiritual insights, our questions and our answers. We need something like global theology.

Theology may not be the best word: it has perhaps too many associations with abstract theorizing and Christian apologetics. But I prefer to use it nevertheless because it appears to be the only word we have for the job in hand, namely, a serious intellectual inquiry into matters of spiritual concern. When theology is doing its job and not being diverted into defensive or abstruse argumentation, it is concerned with the central issues of the day and the central issues of human life itself. It views these in the light of our religious tradition, of course, because the assumption of theology is that human life can only be satisfactorily understood in relation to the ultimate source of our being, what we in the West have usually called God. Strictly speaking, theology is, as the etymology of the word suggests, the study of God, but this has never meant and never could mean that God is the immediate object of observation and study; in theology we try to understand God as the source and basis and ultimate context of our own human existence, and therefore as refracted in human experience and history. It is especially concerned with those responses to life in the past or today which seem to resolve the central problems of life through a knowledge of, or confidence in, the ultimate reality on which our life is based. We can call these responses 'faith' as a kind of shorthand, but faith should then be clearly distinguished from religious beliefs and dogmas which may or may not give expression to faith. Theology could then be described as an attempt to understand the meaning of faith (and doubt as its correlate) in different and changing circumstances. Global theology would be a search for the meaning of faith in the context of our new global situation.

I labour the point for the reason I gave earlier, that if we hope to respond adequately to the present world crisis we need both to cross the boundaries of old religions and ideologies, and to dig deep into the basic religious questions about human identity and security. I would hope people of no religious belief would also find this inquiry important and interesting, for in their agnostic or atheistic way of thinking they may still be looking for faith. I hope to show as well that the old faith of Jesus may acquire a new and challenging meaning in the new situation.

The mention of Jesus raises a point of difficulty, however. The religion that stems from Jesus has been notably silent about the contradictions and failures of Western civilization, apart from a few lonely voices. Its obvious and genuine concern for poverty and racism and preparations for war does not seem to have led to any profound reflections on the causes of these things and their appropriate remedies. (My own conscience has been awakened by religious thinkers of Latin America and India, and by some secular thinkers of Europe like Marx, Fromm and Bahro.) Could it be the case that the Christian church in Europe has been so closely identified over the years with the expansionist project that it is unable to reflect on it critically? It is certainly the case that it offered little opposition to the growth of capitalism, the rapid industrialization of Europe, the venture of imperialism, or the ideology that went with them. On the contrary, it could be argued that it positively supported these ventures, first by encouraging the virtues of money making and private property,[8] and second by its own expansionist project in the shape of the missionary movement. I agree with the Sri Lankan theologian Tissa Balasuriya when he cites as an example of 'theological and spiritual deviation from Jesus Christ ... the church's unquestioned acceptance of the West European model of expansion for its own growth'.[9] And he continues, 'expansion became an ultimate value ... The preaching of the gospel was undertaken for the expansion of the church and, in the case of Catholicism, the subordination of non-European peoples to the Roman pontiff in all matters of religion – and other matters as well.'[10] However, I think it would be foolish to judge the church merely on the basis of that compromise and thereby underestimate its capacity for change. The signs are that the church almost everywhere is becoming more socially conscious and more ready to confront power in the name of spiritual rather than pragmatic values. In any case, it seems to me – and I will have to argue this – that Christianity has within itself, perhaps unbeknown to itself, the resources we need for the present world crisis, not least because it conveys from the past the spiritual wisdom of our own religious heritage. We have much to learn from other religions too – another point I would have to argue – but I suspect we will gain most from them when we can integrate their insights within our own religious tradition. And all this sensitive learning and relearning must be part of our theology.

Having said that I must also say that I am aware of a peculiar temptation that comes to me as a Western theologian. It is as if the failure of Western expansion had made me want to compensate by at least trying to *understand* the whole world, thereby shifting the expansionist impulse into the intellectual sphere! I sincerely hope I can resist the temptation. I am all too well aware, when I am honest with myself, that my view of the world could only be a local view, and of course fragmentary, distorted and limited by my own interests and my own situation. Yet the same would have to be said of people far more knowledgeable than myself. So the enterprise is risky; but it is also, I feel, inevitable and urgent.

TWO

North / South

The present crisis in the economy may seem far removed from any concern of theology, seeming to be an essentially secular affair, until it becomes apparent that economics is entangled in a theology of its own and now, through the crisis, raises deep, theological questions.

The economy can be, and usually is, presented as a reality in its own right, operating according to certain laws or principles which then make it intelligible – in the science of economics – more or less independently of other human realities. With such an economic view we can then grasp the flow of money in the world, the rise and fall of economies, the periodic rises and recoveries and so on without having to refer, for example, to the motivations or ideas or needs of the people involved. A great deal has in fact been written about the functioning of the world economy without any explicit reference to people at all.[1] This can hardly make for good economics. The economy profoundly affects people's behaviour and experience, and these in turn affect the economy, since the economy after all is no more than a system of financial transactions between human beings. A serious crisis in the economy will almost certainly result in a crisis in human affairs – social upheavals, political struggle and so on – and may even issue from such a social or political crisis. The depression of the thirties, to give a simplified example, had something to do with starting the Second World War, and may itself have been caused in part by the First World War. In such cases we cannot really understand what is going on unless we take a wider view than a narrowly economic one.

The present global crisis is such a case. It can be described narrowly, but not so as to answer our deepest worries about it. In strictly financial terms there is, we can say, a cash flow problem: there is a world recession in trade, decline in economic growth, tendencies towards contraction and protectionism, mounting international debt, and a consequent crisis in the international banking system. There are also corresponding policy proposals for dealing with it, including a restructuring of the international economic order.[2] But at the centre of all this stands the tragedy of international debt, and there is a story to be told about this which cannot so easily be contained within the abstractions of economics.

International debt

Few people could have foreseen the oil crisis of the early seventies – brought about by the sudden and dramatic increase in prices (400%) by the oil producing countries – and even less its effects on the world economy. It made the whole manufacturing process more expensive, which put up the price of manufactured goods. In the countries of the South this had two damaging results. The first was that it undermined their own already fragile manufacturing sector which lacked the resources to compete with the obviously more resourceful North. The second is that they could no longer afford the manufactured goods they needed from the North, because of the increase in prices. This happened to coincide with the steep drop in the price of some commodity goods like sugar, which further reduced the power of many poor countries to sell abroad. Their economies threatened to decline into a whirlpool spin.

At this point the IMF (International Monetary Fund) stepped in, followed by commercial banks with money to lend – gained, ironically, from the new profits in oil – to make extra loans to keep the economies of the South going and to help in the payment of interest on aid loans already incurred from the more hopeful age of development. However, the economies of the South have not been revived, so in effect the most severe economic crisis has been only deferred. Meanwhile the debts have been mounting as more loans have to be negotiated to pay off interest on previous loans. (Over this period the rate of interest has been raised unilaterally by countries of the North to protect their own economies.) From the point of view of the IMF further loans can be economically viable only if the debtor countries implement stringent deflationary measures; indeed it has made it a condition of their receiving loans that they should increase their exports to gain more foreign currency and decrease expenditure on home social needs, at whatever cost to their people. Subsidies on basic foods like rice and sugar have therefore been cut, raising food prices by as much as 100%. Further investment in the economy has been curtailed, and government spending on education and welfare has been drastically reduced, to the extent of provoking serious unrest throughout the South, including riot and revolution. The increase in repressive government and dictatorship throughout the world can be seen as a direct result of this new economic stringency.

This is no way to revive an economy, as even the most hardened monetarists will agree. In most Latin American countries poverty has actually increased since 1982 under the pressure of international debt.[3] The most that can be gained from this is that the rich countries will continue to get interest on their commercial loans and aid, and will continue to have resources and markets for their own ailing economies. Is this perhaps why they refuse to take steps to restructure the world economy on the lines set out by economists of the South and by the international Brandt Commission? However that may be, the fact remains that the debts of the poor are presently subsidizing the economies of the rich, and in a whole number of ways, from the payment of interest to the use of loans for the purchase of much needed goods. Even our aid programme to the South is now surpassed by debt payments flowing in the opposite direction.[4]

If the debts aren't written off or rescheduled, as is beginning to happen with some banks, the debtor countries are likely to default in their payments, with very serious consequences for the rest of us. The president of Peru, Alan Garcia, spoke of this recently at the Non-Aligned summit in Harare (September 1986). 'The truth is that the debt of the Third World, the debt of Latin America under present conditions, cannot be paid by any country, for the resulting effort would plunge it into misery and violence.'[5] He then cited the latest figures on the size of the largest debts: Mexico $100 billions, Argentina $50 billions, the Philippines over $30 billions. In the case of Mexico and Brazil the annual repayment and interest amount to one third of their total export earnings. This cruel drainage on resources lowers the capacity of debtor countries to revive their own economies and produce the exports that would enable them to pay: they are caught in a vicious downward spiral. The Brandt Commission summed up the situation in their follow-up report of 1983, *Common Crisis*:

> The developing countries today are, with few exceptions, in a desperate plight. With the prices of commodities – the main exports of many countries – at their lowest level for over thirty years, recession and protectionism affecting their exports of manufactures, a slowing up in the flow of commercial capital and aid, their balance of payments problems have reached intolerable proportions. Cutting back on growth is the order of the day – for those countries which have been growing. For numerous countries – especially in Sub-Saharan Africa, where there has been no growth in recent years – lack of capacity to import translates directly into increased hardship, even threatened starvation, for tens of millions of the most vulnerable people.[6]

It could happen very soon that northern investors will decide to hold back their money because they aren't getting a return – it is already beginning to happen – and/or that southern debtors will refuse to pay because the debts have become damaging and unjust. Either way the results would be catastrophic.

A recent novel by the vice-president of the World Bank, William Clark, paints a vivid and realistic picture of the likely scenario following a major default on debts.[7] The world's banking system would go into crisis because banks would have lent out more than the sum of their assets.[8] Individual banks would call on their creditors, thereby creating a panic in the system, leading to a crash in the already depressed economy.[9] There would, further, be a critical shortage of food and raw materials in the North, since countries of the

South would be desperately reshaping their economies for home use, with the virtual collapse of the modern sector. Delinking from the North, at least in this manner and with this speed, would do irreparable damage both to the North and the South. In this situation piracy and terrorism would be rife. William Clark envisages – quite convincingly to my mind – the formation of a southern terrorist organization which is capable of breaking into the central computer systems of the North and threatening virtually the whole technostructure. He puts the suggestion into the mouth of an African leader who is helping to organize the world-wide resistance:

> 'I believe that we can introduce a new inducement which I will call "inconvenience terror". This will demonstrate that the well-organized, computerized, automatized world of the urban North cannot run smoothly while ignoring and repressing the poor in the outside world and in their midst. This will be particularly effective in England ... You may ask whether we can perform this task. Of course we can. In America there are 15 million citizens of African descent, in Britain 2 to 3 million; and today we have the technical means as never before of mobilizing this force and forging awkward brigades, under the command and instruction of experts, to defy and discommode that white elite which has for so long imposed its will on four-fifths of the world's population.'[10]

The novel ends with a round table conference where leaders of the world, including a chastened British chancellor, try to reshape the world economy in a way that is both just and mutually beneficial.

The idea of a basic restructuring of the economy was the main platform of the influential report *North-South* from Willi Brandt's international commission in 1980, on which, incidentally, William Clark also served. It was a measure that could conceivably be taken by hard-nosed politicians and financiers from both North and South because it appealed to their long-term self-interest. It required no fundamental change of policies, only a determination to make the global system work, which meant, first, unclogging it of unpayable debts – an act of generosity that would soon pay off economically – and second, drawing poorer countries into the decision-making about aid and trade which had previously been the prerogative of the North. It was hoped that a new, genuinely international bank would be set up, in place of the World Bank and the IMF, but linked to the UN, to facilitate the flow of money.

Despite the popular impact of the report and a world conference in Mexico in 1981 no government policies have been changed and no alternative institution has been set up.[11] Rich countries have refused to yield any control of the World Bank and IMF to poorer countries to ensure democratic control. Instead the decline of the world economy has continued, bringing yet more unemployment, social tension and grinding poverty, especially, but not only, in the South.

The development process

The massive loans made to poor countries in the seventies were wholly within the policy established in the forties with the setting up of the World Bank and the IMF and pursued most rigorously in the sixties with the UN Decade of Development. The policy was to stimulate rapid development in the poorer countries of the world – on the model of development already achieved in the North – so that they could participate more fully in the new global economy and enable it to expand. It was believed that the development of the South was not only compatible with that of the North but also necessary to it: that North and South had a mutual interest in an expanding, modern economy.[12] That policy is now called into question, as is the belief that underlies it, with its appalling outcome in the present economic crisis and the ever-widening gap between the rich and the poor. It can no longer be assumed that what has worked for the North should now work for the South as well, or that what works locally can be made to work globally, even from a northern point of view. Then what are we to assume? It is a serious and difficult question because our idea of development in the North has formed an essential part of our idea of progress, which in turn has formed part of our most deeply held belief as people of the modern world. Are we then to assume that our idea of economic development has only a limited range of application? That this typically European idea cannot be made to fit situations that are culturally different from our own? That in imposing anything distinctly our own on the rest of the world we are bound to become part of the problem? Or do we go even further and reject the idea altogether? If we pursue these questions long enough I think we might touch on some deeper questions about ourselves and our relations to others which are inescapably theological.

For one thing we would have to recognize that even the most technically devised schemes of development embody some idea of what it is to be human and to be humanly fulfilled. The barest notion that some improvement in material welfare means an improvement in human welfare says something about what human life is. But what human life is or might be or should be is open to so many possibilities – we hardly dare think about it and mostly we don't. We feel much more secure with notions that are passed on to us ready-made from other people, through the media or our friends or whoever. As a consequence we can hardly imagine other ways to be humanly fulfilled than those we have blithely accepted for ourselves. Even those of us who give time and effort to devising improvements for others are not given much to reflection on what the possibilities of improvements are. A Christian Aid poster some years ago presented the difference between development and underdevelopment as the difference between a smart pair of trousers and a traditional Indian loin cloth. (Christian Aid must have known better than that, but they must have also known that to raise money for development they had to appeal to a European prejudice about what development is.) In development projects and aid programmes, as in so many other activities, we tend to project ourselves on to others, smart trousers and all, and unless they are strong enough to assert themselves with their own distinctive reality we shall continue to regard them as either replicas of ourselves or, if they fail to live up to that image, as unfortunate, inferior beings.

There is another factor. The countries of the North have been remarkably successful in their own grand project of development. Beginning with England in the eighteenth century they have succeeded one by one in overcoming the major problems of structural poverty. Is it possible that our idea of development for the still poor countries of the world is taken directly from our own historical experience? It would not of course be surprising if it were. Where else indeed could we find such a rich source of proven ideas? Yet it has to be recognized that our experience is peculiar in many ways and that the special conditions which made it possible are not always present in other times and places. Much of this has to do with the fact that we pioneered the industrialization project which was to become the very backbone of modern development. We had all the advantages of being first in the field, and although there was also the disadvantage of having to make many first-time mistakes it gave us time to adjust to the great social upheavals that industrialism brought with it.[13] And to some extent, of course, we have retained that advantage. Is our memory in this case selective? Does it tend to reinforce that image of ourselves which makes us feel most comfortable and secure? This suspicion is confirmed by the discovery that the collective memory of our much vaunted progress leaves out almost entirely the story of human suffering which it entailed – this indeed is another set of 'special conditions' which makes our European experience unique. We tend to assume that we in Europe developed out of poverty largely as a result of our own effort and ingenuity, that poverty was and is largely a technical problem for which we discovered an appropriate technical solution, namely a combination of economic planning and technological invention, and that therefore poverty in the world today could in principle be overcome completely by applying the development formula which we have already tried and tested. We need to remind ourselves of those human costs which were not, it would appear, incidental to our development process but an essential part of it. It was of course a complex affair, but I think it is possible to isolate seven factors which were necessary for the take-off of our development process and which continue to be necessary to maintain its momentum.

1. *The accumulation of capital.* This was necessary for the purchase of expensive machinery and plant that made the industrial revolution possible. It was made available from more lucrative methods of exploiting the land, following the enclosures, but more especially from ventures overseas: trade in much-needed spices and foods, the plunder of foreign

treasures (an estimated £25 billion altogether for Europe, according to modern prices), the purchase and sale of some 15 million Africans into slavery (Kuczinski's estimate) giving traders a regular profit of 300% in relation to investment, and later, when the revolution was underway, a profitable trade in manufactured goods in which for a time we maintained a monopoly.

2. *The availability of cheap labour.* If the labour force had been in a position to bargain over wages and conditions the capitalists might never have recouped their investment, or goods would not have been sold at competitive prices. Running costs had to be kept to a minimum. Fortunately for the capitalists there was an endless supply of labour from the impoverished countryside, following the enclosures.

3. *The availability of resources.* Iron and coal were essential at the beginning, and England was generously supplied with them. Water and air were hardly considered as resources at all because they did not have to be paid for. Their value came to be recognized only where they were in short supply or when, as has happened increasingly, they were polluted by the very industrial process they helped to make possible. Other resources could be acquired by trade; we held a strong trading position, backed up when necessary by our superior force at sea and later by military control of the colonies.

4. *The mechanization of production.* This may have been expensive on capital but in the long run it was cheaper from the capitalist's point of view than reliance on labour, although it did lead to unemployment. It also enabled *mass* production which brought the costs down even more. It required a level of science and technical know-how which had only just been achieved in Europe – which is not to deny that science and technology were advanced elsewhere. In this respect as in others the time was ripe for development.

5. *The division of labour.* It was not only cost-efficient, but with mechanization and massification it was inevitable that human work should be degraded to a subjectively meaningless and near mechanical process. The value of work was reduced to the money it earned, creating a new kind of money-materialism, and working people were reduced to a subservient and dependent class.

6. *Control of the markets.* When we alone could produce goods

industrially there was no problem; the cheapness of the goods was sufficient. But with increasing competition from Europe we had to secure our markets as we secured our resources – with military force. Generally, though not always, those who won the war got richer. More recently we have come to rely more on ways of making people want the products we have to sell them, which in its own way requires massive capital investment and technological know-how.

7. *Economic growth.* This is so much a part of the process now that it is thought by many people to be the whole aim of the process. The generation of an overall increase in profits is deemed to be an adequate indication of economic development, regardless of how the money is used or who gets how much of it. Moreover, the pursuit of growth in this narrow sense encourages money-making as a personal and national ambition. However, its essential role in the process of development is to provide ever more capital for further investment; in this way the cycle of industrialism can be maintained. It means nonetheless that production is geared more to the needs of the overall economy than to the specific needs of people in society – unless of course we believe that material growth *is* our prime need.

Collective idolatry

This last point also hints at an explanation for our almost wilful ignorance of past human suffering: that it would call in question the process by which our present wealth and security are acquired and maintained. Our reluctance to accept this dark side of our history can be compared to our reluctance individually to accept the dark side of our own personalities. In both cases we refuse to take on board what cannot be incorporated into our self-image without fundamentally changing our behaviour. In the case of our history we might conveniently forget whatever truth would seriously challenge our present way of life. There might be other reasons to forget: it is after all natural to recall moments of our past that make us proud and give us confidence, and it doesn't do to dwell on failures and wrongs which are now beyond us to repair. But I'm not sure these reasons are sufficient. For to ignore suffering and evil that are part and parcel of the very process on which we pride ourselves is sheer hypocrisy; and to continue to live by that very process and recommend it to others, ignoring the human cost, is surely the worst irresponsibility. How could our sins be so blatant? For we generally believe – I am speaking collectively – that our modern form of development is for the common good, both in Britain and throughout the world: on this point at least there is agreement even between left and right, between East and West. Our ignorance therefore goes much deeper than the mere turning of a blind eye. We seem to be subject to an *illusion* about ourselves and our world which allows us to commit evil while believing we do good.

If we press further still and ask why we should be subject to this illusion, the answer should not be too difficult to discern. Our commitment to progress through industrialism and economic growth is built on the assumption that, as the Bible has it, 'a man's life consists in the abundance of things he possesses', which implies both that material things are the ultimate source of life and that 'possessing' them is the way to obtain and enrich life. It is a basically religious assumption in the sense that it contains an idea of ultimate reality (material things) and a practical proposal for relating to that ultimate reality (through possession and consumption). However, unlike most beliefs that we would recognize as religious it doesn't refer to anything *beyond* this world as a source of its life or significance. Perhaps then we should describe it as a quasi-religion or a tacit religion.[14] The religious character of this commitment is concealed by the secular character of its object. It expresses a religious attitude to the material world itself, which in most religions is either rejected or relativized. To be more precise – since there is very little reverence for nature here – we should say that it adopts this attitude to usable matter and to the material products humans have made for their use. As in the religions of magic, it is a relationship in which humans, while expressing their dependency, retain power and control, at least through their powerful representatives. In this quasi-religion the possession of goods is meant to give one security and strength and status, i.e. value in the sight of others. The consumption of goods is meant to satisfy one's basic needs. The buying of a desired product is like a worldly sacrament, conveying through each single material transaction the meaning of one's life as a whole. The truth about this semi-divine reality will be revealed through the meticulous study of matter in so far as it is usable and manipulable, namely through modern science, which has indeed become the over-riding orthodoxy of our culture. Hope for the resolution of the conflicts and miseries of life – redemption – will be invested in the disciplined application of our scientific knowledge to the material problems underlying our misery and in the systematic acquisition of material wealth that can solve these problems. With such a quasi-religious hope it is quite natural to believe that the misery of world poverty can be overcome by the relentless pursuit of economic growth.

Once we have expressed it in this form we can recognize that as a religion it is inadequate and deformed, for it takes as ultimate what is in fact only relative and partial, and it must therefore finally disappoint those who rely on it. In the biblical sense this worship of things-to-be-possessed is idolatry. Idolaters, according to the prophet Isaiah, 'do not know, nor do they discern ... No one considers, nor is there knowledge or discernment to say, "Half of it [the wood] I burned in the fire, I also baked bread on its coals, I roasted flesh and have eaten; and shall I make the residue of it an abomination? Shall I fall down before a block of wood?"' (44.18f.); according to the apostle Paul, 'although they knew God they did not honour him as God or give thanks to him, but they became futile in their thinking and their senseless minds were darkened ... They exchanged the truth about God for a lie and worshipped and served the creature rather than the Creator' (Rom. 1.21, 25).

Inevitably the pursuit of one aspect of life as if it were the whole leads to imbalance, blindness and suffering. Above all, to treat limited material resources as if they were everything we needed is to encourage a competitive and exploitative mode of life such as in fact we have in the industrialized West: hence the suffering of the poor of the world who have come to depend on us but cannot compete with us; hence too the illusion which must protect us from the awful truth of our collective idolatry.

Suffering has a power to reveal truths to us which we would otherwise refuse to consider, especially when it is our own suffering, but possibly also when it is the suffering of others who are innocent. It confronts us with the reality we have been trying to avoid in our pursuit of an illusion. It may simply *be* the experience of that reality, as when we suffer from neglect of our own bodies. This was an on-going theme of the Old Testament prophets who appealed to the suffering of their people, or to their likely suffering in future, to remind them of the truths of their fundamental identity as a 'people of God'. Their suffering was ascribed ultimately to the folly or faithlessness or plain ignorance which had led them to put their trust in an idol such as military power or a fertility goddess instead of the ultimate source of life, Yahweh. Suffering enabled them to recognize again that the only thing worthy of trust was the very un-thing-like reality that had brought everything, including them, into being, elusive and intangible though it was.

This old tradition of the prophets could shed light on our present situation, if we accept – what I argued before – that the suffering of the poor of the world and our own possible suffering call in question the fundamental commitments of our modern way of life. It raises a particular question about what it is we ultimately trust, and for what kind of benefit or security. And in emphasizing that it introduces the idea of a reality transcending the world, and so transcending everything we normally and naturally put our trust in when confronted with insecurity or uncertainty. The name by which that reality was known to the prophets may seem strange to us now, unless we are deeply nurtured in that tradition, and even then it will seem strange in other contexts where the tradition is not known. But this should not be too serious a problem. The other gods and idols of that time are also strange to us; but we can recognize their equivalent in the gods and idols of our own time, although they carry very different names. But more importantly, in recognizing the idols of our time *as* idols, that is, as mere objects with a pretence of finality, we can understand more clearly what this ultimate and final reality must be, which no name, not even God, can adequately refer to. It is an insight into the truth that 'a man's life' does not consist in 'the abundance of things he possesses', but on the contrary, consists in a quite non-possessive, non-clinging relationship with everything and everyone; and that the openness and courage of such a relationship can only come from a deep confidence in the process of life as a whole.

With such an insight it should be possible to envisage a way of life that was not essentially exploitative or competitive, that is, a way of life in which the enrichment of some did not necessarily entail the impoverishment of others, which positively affirmed, therefore, the unity and interdependence of human life as a whole. That would mean at the very least a social life that was economically just. Whether such a life could be lived in practice, or has been so lived, is another matter, of course, but the resolve to live it 'if possible' seems to be essential to any religious commitment that expresses a fundamental trust in God or the transcendent. In all the major religions there is a clear indication that letting go of material things is a precondition of genuine faith in God. In the teaching of Jesus it is presented as a straightforward choice: 'No one can serve two masters; for either he will hate the one and love the other, or he will be devoted to the one and despise the other. You cannot serve God and Mammon' (Matt. 6.24).

The main burden of Jesus' teaching was that the choice between the present order of the world and the emerging new order of God, the 'kingdom of God', was being forced on people by the events of their time. The old, oppressive order was beginning to crumble, and there were 'signs', however small, that it was coming to an end, making way for the freedom and harmony of the new world order. Is it possible that in our own time the tragedy of the economic crisis is a 'sign of the kingdom of God'?

THREE

East / West

The most obvious global worry in the rich countries of the world is not in their relations with the poor countries of the South but in relations between themselves, between East and West. For here there is a more immediate and tangible threat in the shape of a possible nuclear war. It is more tangible in that it more directly concerns us, it is more easily imaginable – as imaginable at any rate as our own immediate death – and it is already prepared, down to the very last detail. Despite the recent thaw of attitudes, most of the armaments are still in place. They are at the ready, as if war had already been declared, as if we had set out deliberately to stage Armageddon on a global scale. This of course is not the case, and no such scenario is intended, at least consciously. It is argued that our deployment of nuclear weapons is intended precisely to deter any such eventuality and that in so far as it does so it guarantees our security. But the gap between readiness and intention is one of the strangest and most worrying facts of this new situation. It is a gap that could so easily be closed – it is a relatively simply political decision. This security policy has taken us, necessarily it would seem, perilously close to the very disaster it is intended to avert.

The situation is highly paradoxical. The conflict has reached a point – we could also say the history of human conflict has reached a point – where the construction of a defence becomes the greatest source of danger even to those defending. The conflict is therefore not only extremely dangerous for the world, but also extremely puzzling. How can we begin to understand it?

The nature of the East/West conflict

The conflict is in some respects familiar, at least to those of us who have any experience or knowledge of the last World War, for then the great European nations battled among themselves for world domination. In the event they were so weakened by the struggle that none achieved it. It was America and Russia – I will use these strictly incorrect names because they are publicly perceived in this way and public perception is so much a part of the conflict – which emerged as the new world powers. But significantly they were themselves originally European peoples who had expanded to the West and the East respectively to colonize vast underdeveloped territories. Their rise to world dominance after World War II was yet another manifestation of European expansionism. And as in the previous European conflicts of this century, their expansion has led to an inevitable conflict as they compete with each other for the available space. The political scientist James O'Connell recently summarized the situation as follows:

> In essence the conflict between them [the USA and the USSR] arises out of the way that the world has grown suddenly small. Both powers straddle the same space with little in world history or their own regional or state histories to assist them in dealing with space that is common and for which nearly all history suggests that they should compete.[1]

Their geo-political expansion has been matched by an equally dramatic economic expansion, which has enabled them in turn to invest massively in the technology of war, giving them an undisputed military supremacy in the world. In a sense they have only each other to fear.

They are not, however, competing directly for pieces of territory. There is no real expectation – at least on the part of governments and the military – of any side invading the other, although propaganda may lead us to think otherwise. In the West the evocation of the Russian Threat has had more to do with the needs of ideology than those of military security. That is to say, the portrayal of the communist East as a dangerous enemy has helped governments of the West, and especially America, to win support for their own economic expansion into the rest of the world.[2] In this respect Western expansion is different from that of the East. It aims unashamedly at dominating and exploiting the world's resources and the world's markets in order to achieve an ever-increasing economic growth. Russia, on the other hand, has little need and little occasion to venture into the wider world. It has sufficient resources for development within its own hinterland. If Russia is expansionist it is in respect of its hope for world socialism. Yet it would be a serious oversimplification to suppose that Soviet foreign policy was governed by a concern for the world mission of socialism, for that concern has been increasingly balanced and checked by a concern to prevent war. Since its birth in the revolution of 1917 it has been 'encircled' by nations who wished to undermine it or destroy it. The devastating experience of World War II, in which 20 million Soviet citizens lost their lives, has left the country with a deep disgust of war and a strong determination to protect itself militarily against any such incursion from hostile countries. This psychological factor helps to explain why the Soviet Union has poured such vast resources into nuclear arms so as to maintain parity with the United States. By the same token, as we shall see later, the Soviet Union has come to think twice about the nuclear arms race since this in its own way also threatens peace.[3]

So far the conflict is not so different from the many that preceded it. But the present conflict is new in other respects, some of which, it has to be said, are *so* new that we are mostly at a loss how to deal with them. Consider four of them.

1. *The geographical scale.* America is already cut off from the rest of the world by two large oceans, encouraging an isolationist approach, and that despite its concern to lead the world in its own great cause. Russia is cut off by choice, to protect its own unique economic and social structure from invasion by capitalist seduction. Having embroiled so many other nations in the conflict, they have complicated it immensely. The size and distances involved have raised the stakes, encouraged fear and fantasy at the strangeness of other cultures in remote parts of the globe, and through these reduced the possibility of a mutual understanding that could help to resolve the conflict.

2. *The ideological gap.* Partly because of their geographical

27

remoteness, America and Russia have had the freedom to develop quite different economic, social and political systems, both of which, as it happens, grew out of revolutions with a clear ideological significance. Both had links in fact with the French Revolution of 1789, yet they each developed distinctive interpretations of revolution and each continues to identify itself in terms of that interpretation. If *liberté* became the dominant idea in the West, it was *égalité* in the East. Those differences were further heightened by the social conflict in nineteenth century Europe which gave birth to the opposing ideologies of capitalism and socialism. On top of that again the West has chosen to regard itself as culturally Christian, whilst the East, folowing Marx's and Engels' interpretation of socialism, chose to regard itself as atheist – yet again, an old European conflict was projected on to the world at large. Each became a mirror image of the other, and defined itself in opposition to the other. Is it any wonder that the superpowers find it so difficult to communicate, yet so easy to condemn?

3. *The destructive potential.* As a result of rapid economic growth on both sides and a series of rapid developments in technology, the power of their weaponry has increased immeasurably. The creation of a bomb that could destroy whole cities brought an end to that era when nations could expect to deploy their full force in warfare, for the new bomb was not only capable of destroying far more than could ever be morally acceptable, at least by the norms of a 'just war', but its use would invite a retaliation that would amount to collective suicide. This new factor had a positive possibility. It could motivate nations to seek alternatives to war as a way of resolving conflict: the United Nations in particular gained momentum from this. It could also be deployed as a purely deterrent weapon – although 'weapon' is an odd word for a capability that is not intended for actual use – that would protect a country from any military attack whatever: Nobel's dream of an absolute security from an absolute deterrent. The defence policies of both sides have indeed been built on this premiss. The traditional policies in defence, by which a country gains military supremacy and/or economic dominance, were officially abandoned in favour of the new deterrence policy. But it cannot be said that the new policy has given us

an absolute security or anything like it. Nuclear deterrence obviously breeds suspicion and fear as much as it makes us feel secure. Against the fear that one side would be overwhelmed by the other they resorted on both sides to the older form of material security, namely the struggle for dominance. The fusion of these two forms of security, effective deterrence and military supremacy, has fired an arms race which has greatly increased the potential damage, and risk, of a nuclear exchange. Also, the invention and construction of intermediate nuclear weapons has broken the 'firebreak' which had made an escalation from conventional to nuclear war virtually impossible. Together with the proliferation of nuclear weapons and the formation of such military alliances as NATO and the Warsaw Pact with joint nuclear policies these developments have created a destructive potential that far outreaches anything known before and indeed any conceivable military requirement.

4. *The industrial connection.* 40% of our national budgets and 50% of our scientific resources, both human and material, are devoted, directly or indirectly, to the defence programme,[4] which therefore provides the basis for a secure, well-founded and expanding business. The commitment of so much of a country's economy to the arms race makes it extremely difficult to put it into reverse.

The effect of these new factors in the conflict is to have made it highly volatile and dynamic. Deterrence works on stalemate, which we have never had. So, despite stated policy, deterrence also stimulates the conflict by fuelling the arms race. There is a reciprocal process here, not simply in the accumulation of arms, but also in the perception of danger. Deterrence goes into reverse when e.g. another advance in nuclear capability is perceived, not unreasonably, as an act of aggression. Eact act of aggression has then to be matched by a similar act of defence/aggression, and so on in an apparently unending process. Hence the notorious ambiguity of all nuclear weaponry. Hence the very widespread perception that nuclear deterrence is potentially *self*-destructive – which has led, oddly enough, to two quite incompatible attitudes: the refusal of the peace movement and the 'subjective exterminism' of the right.[5]

This frighteningly new and hardly comprehensible dynamic

is now also compounded with older and more familiar elements of conflict of a psychological nature which make the situation more complex than ever. We have noted the psychological effect of distance between the superpowers, that it makes it all too easy to imagine the worst of this strange, remote enemy. It is not of course unreasonable, as I have said, to see the large and accumulating range of missiles on the other side as a serious threat to our safety. It is quite something else, though, to see the other side as the one and only source of this horrific violence, for this is obviously to deny the equal potential of violence on our side. Irrational as it may be, it is psychologically compelling, for the potential for violence in our own nuclear arsenals is not something we can easily accept if we wish to retain a sense of our being good and right, and we *have* to retain this sense of ourselves in order to justify our possession of these weapons as a deterrent. This works psychologically for the other side as well: on both sides there are vicious (interlocking) circles from which it is very difficult to escape. Each adopts a military posture which can match the apparently more threatening posture of the other. But this in its own way is so threatening to human life, so far beyond anything we humans could accept morally or emotionally if we were ever to carry out the threat, that we mask our own violence and project it on to the other. Such tricks of the mind obscure the situation even further, calling for an even more irrational response. The psychiatrist, Jeremy Holmes, describes the process in this way:

> Each of the superpowers sees in its opponent an image of its own ambition, expansionism and desire for absolute superiority. This terrifying vision of the enemy then fuels the race for more fearsome deterrents on each side. In the atmosphere of mutual projection it is impossible for each side realistically to assess the threat which the other poses. For example, commentators seem to have great difficulty in gauging the likelihood of a Russian invasion of Great Britain. If each side were able to acknowledge its *own* wish to attack and humiliate the enemy, rather than steadfastly insisting that its armaments were merely defensive, it might then be easier to look at how great the actual threat

is, and whether it is more or less dangerous than possessing nuclear weapons.[6]

Reagan's depiction of the Soviet Union as 'an evil empire' and the 'focus of evil' and his call to the British Houses of Parliament in 1983 for a global crusade against communism exemplify this outlook dramatically.[7] We should add that such projections also serve to strengthen a leader's position at home and with his allies, and more importantly, that they confirm the self-identity of a people by contrasting it with the Other who is different and dangerous. Machiavelli advised his 'prince', when confronted with dissension among his people, to make war with an enemy, and Shakespeare's Henry IV advised his son, who was to succeed him and inherit a nest of quarrels, 'Therefore, my Harry, be it thy course to busy giddy minds with foreign quarrels.' The advice has been well heeded by the princes of America and Russia, who have inherited large, disunited empires with little sense of a continuing cultural identity. What they lacked from history they have gained from the cold war.[8]

Given what we know about an international conflict like this, with such a capacity for self-perpetuation, it is hard to believe that it can be resolved in any way short of military confrontation, and yet for reasons given such a confrontation also seems unthinkable. Those who give any attention to it are likely to be filled with a most awful sense of inevitability.

The spiritual dimension of the conflict

In an important sense, however, it is not like other conflicts. We have already noted that the impossibility of resolving it through military means has led people on both sides to think of alternative possibilities, and in the case of the UN, for example, to develop alternative institutions. The agreement on 18 September 1987 to abandon short-range and medium-range nuclear missiles (confirmed by the INF Treaty later that year), for the first time putting the arms race into reverse, is a promising indication that this new way of thinking is affecting real policy. This real reduction in arms, albeit a mere 4% of the total, has in turn had a psychological effect in the perception of the conflict. A change is already taking place in the Soviet Union. As many as five years ago a senior figure in the party secretariat, Georgi Shahnazarov, published an article which challenged the traditional approach to foreign and defence policy. It read, 'In the nuclear age, war can no longer be considered as a means for achieving political objectives ... There are no political objectives that could justify the use of means that could lead to nuclear war'.[9] On 16 February 1987 Gorbachev himself gave voice to this new philosophy in his remarkable speech to the Peace Forum in Moscow. He said:

> We do not know the ultimate truth – our national reconstruction is an invitation to any social system to compete with socialism peacefully. We will be able to prove in practice that such competition benefits universal progress and world peace ... Our desire to make our own country better will hurt no one, with the world only gaining from this ... [There was a long debate in the Soviet leadership] before we saw things as they are, and became convinced that new approaches and methods are required for resolving international problems in today's complex and contradictory world, a world at the crossroads ... We came to conclusions that made us review something that once seemed axiomatic, since after Hiroshima war, at least world war, ceased to be the continuation of state policy by other means ... The nuclear powers must step out from the nuclear shadow, and enter a nuclear free world, thus ending the alienation of politics from the general human norms of ethics.[10]

But the matter goes deeper than this, and has to if the hopes of Gorbachev and others are to be realized. For to abandon war we have to abandon the violent postures and confrontations that lead to war, and, by the same logic, the economic and political ambitions which make the other side a threat. The possibility of nuclear war calls into question the social attitudes and practices that have brought it about. To remove that possibility we need a very fundamental change of attitude. But to speak in this fashion, it might be felt, is surely to slip into a kind of spiritual idealism which is quite inappropriate in the world of politics. Surely here, more than anywhere, we need to be studiously realistic. This doubt is inevitable, but it misses one all-important factor in the situation, one of those new and hardly comprehensible factors which make it different from anything we have known till now.

It is the fact that the threat posed by this conflict is a threat of global extinction. In this sense we are close to the end. To use the theological term, we are confronting the *eschaton*. And the awareness that we are close to the end, because at any time we could bring the end about, has a profound effect – if we allow it to, and even to some extent if we don't – on our awareness of ourselves and the world in general. It gives us, to begin with, an awesome sense of our responsibility, for it is finally up to us whether we and our world survive. That is a hard truth to take on board, and many people no doubt are suppressing the thought to avoid anxiety.[11] But whether we accept it or not, it is impossible to avoid its impact once we have realized, even for a moment, the implications of the nuclear threat. It will work on us subconsciously if we don't allow it to do otherwise, creating an unfocussed dread that saps our energy and hope. There is already much evidence that most young people in the modern world are gloomy about the future because of it. But however negative its impact might be, however inadequate our response to it, it must at least have some impact on the feelings and attitudes that fuel the global conflict. The threat of extinction has an ultimacy that overrides all other concerns, challenging us to re-evaluate our lives and the meanings we have given them. Although it appears at first to bear a wholly negative significance, it seems to have the power, through its effect on our consciousness, to awaken us spiritually.

It is not, I think, fanciful to compare this situation with that of an individual in a mid-life crisis. In that individual experience we may be made more starkly aware of ourselves by the realization that we must inevitably die. In one sense we are aware of this for most of our lives, but it is not a fact that has to impinge on everyday life, since to all intents and purposes, especially in youth, we can live life as if it went on forever. In mid-life it often becomes apparent – through illness, the death of a parent or the mere process of aging – that our death does impinge on our life in the present, and that in doing so it makes every moment irreplaceable, every achievement and ambition questionable, every individual person unique. Human life is seen to be precious, fragile and ambivalent. It is now up to us, we may feel, what we make of it, whether it is filled with meaning and value or dissolves into emptiness. We may feel especially aware of our bodies as finite entities that deserve to be cared for: the thought of death in this case may encourage us positively to affirm life. It gives us at least a new power of choice, a new freedom. Old habits of thought and practice lose their power over us as we see them in the light of an impending death. In that respect death makes a gift of freedom.

A mid-life crisis is often associated, for those who are inclined that way, with a deepening religious awareness. It may be the experience of finitude and transience, where nothing at all can ultimately be relied on, which turns us to look for something more secure. It may be the experience of unfulfilled dreams or broken ideals that makes us look for an inner healing or reconciliation. Carl Jung described this phase of life as a quest for individuation, and noted that no patient of his who had been psychologically troubled in mid-life had managed to resolve that trouble without discovering or rediscovering a religious sense of life.

I can see a reflection of this familiar experience in the new situation of nuclear threat in which whole (and global) collectivities are being traumatized by the knowledge of death. It is almost as if a new truth is being disclosed which in our relative immaturity we are finding hard to accept. Yet, if we do accept, it offers us also a new kind of freedom.

It is of course natural to regard the prospect of mass death as utterly gloomy, too horrific even to contemplate, and seriously thought about only by people of an unhealthy disposition. But since the prospect is in fact quite realistic, given the state of the East/West conflict, and since it has everything to do with the way we conduct our lives and our politics now, it would seem to be also very *un*natural not to dwell on it. It could be itself an unhealthy attitude to evade and repress such an all-pervasive reality.[12] But more importantly – and this to my mind gives theological significance to the threat – it can, through our contemplation, create the conditions for faith and hope beyond its awful negativity.

And finding such a positive possibility in this mask of death can help us, as nothing else can, to face its reality. The two seem to be reciprocally related: our readiness to find hope in the prospect of mass extinction enables us to face up to its dark reality; and our facing up to it courageously enables us to find hope.

The hope is grounded in the power of the *eschaton* to disclose the truth, to clarify our moral choice and to free us from some all-too-comfortable illusions and self-centred practices. (This may seem a great deal to claim for a mere possibility, but the possibility is inherent in our present way of life and is only mirrored back to us by the future. It shows us nothing that we couldn't also have learned by looking.) It allows no way out, no escape from the one route that will lead to our salvation. It confronts us with death and futility at the end of every path except the one that will remove the occasion of the threat. It gives us a stark choice about our future, not only in theory but also in the practical sense that it forces us to rethink our basic options and to abandon our confidence in what we took to be the inevitable tendency of human behaviour. We do not after all have to be fatalistic about the conflict because it relies on human attitudes and responses from which we can, if we wish, wholly dissociate ourselves. What we took to be inevitable because of a 'realistic' idea of human nature – irredeemably selfish and greedy, perhaps – turns out *not* to be inevitable, so long as a deeper or larger truth impinges upon us.

A larger truth does impinge on us when we allow the implications of the *eschaton* to sink in. It becomes clear that the collective attitudes we have pursued until now are self-defeating, that although we thought in all honesty that we were pursuing the interests of security and peace we were in fact pursuing policies that systematically undermined them. To be more specific, we have been profoundly misled on three counts.

1. We have supposed that our security lies ultimately in possessing enough material power to fend off any attack from outside. It leaves out of account altogether the in-security that such a posture creates by undermining our relationships with other people. Our reliance specifically on the technological power to destroy displays both too much

confidence in material power and too little trust in our fellow human beings. Since all else virtually has been sacrificed to the erection of the all-powerful Weapon it must be described and denounced as a modern idol. We are expecting of it far more than it is capable of giving, and we must recognize the illusion of its power for what it is. Indeed, by putting all our trust in it we are turning it into a demonic and destructive force.

2. In ensuring that *we* survive we have presumed that 'we' refers to our own country, or perhaps more generously, the West. But it has now been made clear by the possibility of Mutual Assured Destruction that we cannot protect ourselves at the expense of others. Even the first strike capability, which would supposedly pre-empt a counter attack, would, if used, create ecological disaster for all of us, the so-called 'nuclear winter' from which none will survive. The relatively minor accident at Chernobyl – minor for a nuclear accident – made it clear to everyone, or should have, that we live in the same world and that disasters for one side are also disasters for the other. Our fates are now tied together, East and West, and if we really seek security it will have to be a 'common security'[13] that includes all nations. If instead we put our own nation first and are prepared to sacrifice other peoples' for the sake of it we would, to use a phrase of Francis Bacon's, make 'an idol of the tribe'.

3. We have assumed that economic expansion through further industrialization is essential to our welfare. But, as we have seen in the case of the North/South relationship, this can be secured only at great human cost. In the case of the East/West relationship the cost is felt in the competition for global hegemony, in the proxy wars around the globe that waste lives and resources, in the soaring expenses of the arms race, and finally in the Russian roulette that puts all our lives at risk. To pursue increasing material wealth even at this cost is, to use another phrase of Bacon's, to make 'an idol of the market place'.

The dread of the nuclear *eschaton* gnaws at our confidence in these long-standing idols of the modern world. It fills us with a kind of nausea at having wasted so much of our collective effort on these seductive but fruitless concerns. But there is another dread even beyond this: that there is after all nothing worthy of our trust and effort. Does the nuclear *eschaton* then expose the futility of *all* human concern?

Theological response

There is, so far as I can see, no obvious religious consolation here, though the situation does seem to call for it. Many religious people have found it possible in the past to believe in the coming of God's kingdom because they could see how other 'kingdoms' that were set up in rivalry and *hubris* would inevitably crumble, and that out of the ashes a new, purer form of life would emerge, centred more on the hidden reality of God. But since we can now envisage the destruction of the world – even, hypothetically, the destruction of the universe – this form of hope no longer seems possible. The most we are left with in contemplating the nuclear end is the confidence that the God who created us will be able to create again. But there is no content to this hope, and nothing of us that can be thought to survive. Also, the very possibility of our destroying the world suggests that a power that we once ascribed to God has fallen into our own finite hands.[14] Does this mean – to think in traditional terms – that God is no longer in control of the situation? Was God ever? If we trust in God, what precisely are we trusting God to do?

These last questions may contain within themselves the seeds of an answer. They betray an attitude to God based on the certainty that, if God exists and is trustworthy, God will *do* something, that whatever *we* do God will see to it that it will all come out right. Expressed in these terms it is evidently a rather childish belief, and with two startling and, I think, wholly unacceptable implications: that whatever we do makes no difference to the ultimate outcome, which means that we are not finally responsible for the consequences of our actions; and that we can therefore look to God as an absolute security against death and disaster, freeing us from having to worry about what might happen to other people or to ourselves as a result of our actions. In both respects God's sovereignty is being construed so as to undermine human responsibility – as in the old doctrine of predestination. In the face of this new threat nothing could be more *ir*responsible than to sponsor such an idea of God, not least because it would provide an easy argument for 'subjective exterminists' who feel in need of a religious justification. There is, unfortunately, some warrant for religious fatalism in the biblical writings known as apocalyptic, a genre that was developed at a time of extreme despair and helplessness. It is perhaps indicative of the despair felt by many people today that they find themselves so powerfully drawn to this apocalyptic thinking.[15] The prophetic message, on the other hand, was addressed to those who still have power to act; and its promise is conditional: *if* you change, then you will be saved, otherwise you will die a death of your own doing. This does, admittedly, place the responsibility firmly back in the hands of frail human beings, and if applied to the nuclear situation, it allows for the possibility that human beings will in their irresponsibility bring their world to an end. Does it also then remove God from the situation and leave us ultimately nothing to trust? This would appear to be the case, I think, only to those who regard God as a being outside the world who acts on our lives by intervening in and/or controlling our situation. But this is at best a very limited concept of God, since it quite fails to come to terms with the qualitative difference of God's reality as infinite and unlimited. If God is viewed rather as the ultimate reality that impinges on us – in different ways in different situations – we can recognize God here in the reality of our new ultimate responsibility. We have been given a godlike power over life and death, a power to create and to destroy. We have also been given – or should I say, offered – grace to affirm life in and through the situation itself. For there is real grace in being enabled to act by the revelation of the hidden possibilities of a new order of life, where humans take responsibility for one another and their world. This hidden kingdom of God is a mystery: it is there for those who wish to see it and to respond. Moreover, in responding to this hidden possibility which is continually offered us, but most dramatically now in the mirror of the *eschaton*, we actualize the kingdom and participate in the creative power by which we ourselves and our world came into being.

To live in hope of a new world, made new by the renunciation of idols and the affirmation of one another, is to act creatively in the face of possible destruction. It is not to live with a certainty about the future, or with a guarantee of safety for oneself or for any one else. On the contrary, the possibility of loss and of death has to be fully embraced so that the creative affirmation becomes fully possible. Then, in the creative affirmation it will be clear that this is the power of God, expressing itself in and through us; and our life then gains meaning, not through its endless prolongation, but in uniting with the source of our life in the present moment.

Practical response

The response would have to be practical if it was to establish a firm meaning for our lives in the shadow of the *eschaton*. Most obviously it will be aimed at removing the occasion of war. But we have also seen that this goal will require a fundamental shift of personal and social attitudes if it is to be realized. It will mean in fact that the possible new order that we can envisage now would become the inspiration for our life and activity now. We should be doing what Jesus had urged his own people to do: to enter the kingdom of God here and now.

There is however one general difficulty in applying the teaching of Jesus to our global situation, although in its own way it may be illuminating too. Jesus made radical demands on those who wished to follow him, or rather he made it clear that the eschatalogical situation made radical demands on them. Some people, for example, were expected to give up their property. Others had to abandon work and family. But everyone had to change in some way. That general demand could be summarized as follows.

1. A disciple – follower – must abandon everything and everyone he or she is attached to for the sake of the kingdom. And serving the interests of the kingdom carried the implication of not serving the interests of other kingdoms, such as the Roman Empire. 'Render unto Caesar the things that are Caesar's and to God the things that are God's', which has an obvious relevance to the gobal kingdoms of our own day.

2. Even the Samaritan is to be regarded as a neighbour. A disciple cannot afford the psychological luxury of enemies. So-called 'enemies' must be treated as neighbours, so that enmity can be overcome.

3. 'Resist not evil' – with force, I presume. Rather than 'take

up the sword' a disciple must be ready to die, to 'take up the cross'. Evil is to be overcome by other means than violence.

4. If it was customary for people to 'lord it over one another', achieving security by gaining the upper hand, this was not to be the case with his disciples. They were to put themselves at the disposal of others, like the Son of Man who 'came not to be served but to serve and to give his life as a ransom for many'.

But is it to be expected that governments and other collectivities will give the least attention to Jesus' radicalism? Hardly. So how then can it be relevant? We may at least hope that they will gain some insight into our global situation and how they might respond to it from the example of a few courageous people who do dare to follow Jesus. But also, there does seem to be a form of response which fits the nature of collectivities. If the demand of individual disciples of Jesus was that to gain life they should 'deny themselves' for the benefit of others, we could say that the implication for collectivities, who cannot in the nature of the case deny themselves, is that to gain life in the modern world they should at least put the interests of other groups on a par with their own.[16] In Jesus' time the imminence of God's kingdom put everyone in the same boat – everyone would be brought to account before God in the very near future on the issue of whether they supported the kingdoms of this world or the hidden kingdom of God. In our own time, we could say, peoples are being called to account by the imminent crisis of collective destruction, and the question that is being posed is whether they are putting forward their own interests at the expense of others' and therefore at the expense of the whole, or whether indeed they are pursuing the interest of the whole. Jesus' reaffirmation of the old law to 'love your neighbour as yourself' takes on a new and urgent meaning in the confrontation of the superpowers, but that meaning has also to be somewhat diluted or translated so that it can become a practical possibility for nations and power blocs. If we cannot 'love our enemies' *en masse* we can at least recognize them as fellow human beings, hold them in respect, listen to their point of view, and acknowledge their needs and interests, since our interests and theirs are ultimately identical.

In what sense is this a practical alternative to present policies of peace and security? It cannot be claimed that it will guarantee our security in the way it was hoped deterrence would. But then we have discovered that our confidence in an absolute deterrent was misplaced, that it was indeed idolatrous, since it looked for an absolute assurance in a human construction that had all the fallibility of the humans who made it. Evidently, it is part of the hard truth we are being forced to confront that no such absolutes are to be found and that the quest for them can only be delusory and destructive. What is left for us is to look for our security in our relationship with those people who apparently threaten us. Building respect and mutual interest between people will create a kind of trust that will make us feel, as well as be, very much safer. Not that we can guarantee our safety here either, since with humans there will always be uncertainty and surprise. But if we can believe that building trust tends to evoke positive responses, we can commit ourselves to it with some hope. And if, at a deeper level, we can trust the source of our common life which we experience in the creative process of reconciling enemies, we can live with the possibility of defeat and death since these no longer deprive our lives of all meaning. Their meaning lies, after all, in the affirmation of what we are, and what we all are together.

FOUR

People / Planet

The ecological crisis is not nearly so obvious or so clearly focussed as either of the other global crises we have considered. Compared with them it works slowly, silently and in many different and apparently unconnected ways. It appears at one time as a famine in Africa, then as an accident at a nuclear power station, and again as a rise in the incidence of cancer. It does not crystallize into a single situation, nor does it threaten us with a single cataclysmic event.

For this reason it has often been taken less seriously. Those who do take it seriously have often been criticized for diverting our time and attention from the more pressing social problems of poverty and war, for pandering to the sensitivities of middle-class people who are upset by the blots on their landscape, for indulging in ecological sentimentality when they cannot face the hard facts of modern life, and for pining for the imagined simplicities of the pre-industrial past. These criticisms may in many cases be fair, but in general they imply a far too superficial view of the ecological crisis itself, which amounts to something far larger and deeper than specific problems with the natural environment. The recent rapid growth of the green movement indicates that more and more people are becoming aware of this.

Levels of crisis

The specific ecological issues which have caught the public imagination and concern could be grouped into four broad areas, although these are, it has to be admitted, very different in character:

1. There is first of all, and perhaps most noticeably, the *pollution* of the earth from increased industrial activity. What is in common between the fouling of the seas from nuclear waste, the destruction of temperate forest from acid rain, the warming of the earth by the greenhouse effect, the poisoning of the soil through the use of fertilizers and insecticides is that in each process the delicate balances of nature are being upset by the invasion of man-made chemicals which are foreign to it and which it is not able to absorb. This generalization does need to be qualified, however, because not all intrusive matter is strictly speaking invented by human beings. Mercury, for example, is perfectly 'natural' in its place, but if it intrudes into living organisms, and especially if it passes through the food chain, its presence is very damaging. Similarly, carbon dioxide is quite natural, and indeed necessary, in limited proportions, but when large amounts of it are injected into the atmosphere it upsets the delicate balance of gasses which is necessary for the sustenance of life. Pollution, as Barry Commoner puts it, is essentially matter in the wrong place. Pollution in this sense is therefore rather more serious than the fouling of beaches that upset would-be bathers or even the creation of smog which threatens people's health, since it affects the whole fabric of the earth on which our life depends.[1]

2. The *erosion* of the soil is another broad category, which covers the loss of fertility in the normally rich soils of Europe and the loss of soil itself in the ecologically fragile areas of the South. The pressures on soil are various, but the one consistent factor is a persistant overuse of the soil without regard for its ecological limits. The rate at which topsoil is disappearing makes for an alarming prognosis. Even Europe is losing nearly one billion tonnes of soil a year, while Asia, the worst area, is losing as much as 25 billion tonnes. If this process continues we shall find that all the new land that is to be cultivated in the next twenty years to cope with a larger populaton will be matched by the amount of land lost through erosion.[2]

3. The so-called 'energy crisis' derives from the *depletion* of natural non-renewable resources we have come to rely on almost exclusively in our expanding industrial economy, namely, oil, coal and gas. The ecological side of the problem is simple: there is a limited stock of the fossil fuels under the

earth and at the rate at which they are now being used they will soon – probably early in the next century – be used up. What makes the matter critical for us is that we have developed our industrial civilization on the assumption that the energy sources to fuel it are limitless. (It is perhaps some small comfort, however, that the loss of these fossil fuels will be ecologically beneficial in so far as the burning of them is a major source of pollution.)

4. With pollution and erosion, which can destroy whole habitats for some forms of life, and particularly with the destruction of the tropical rain forests, there is a progressive *annihilation* of species of both animal and vegetable life. The present rate of extinction is now about one species a day. By the end of the century, it is estimated, we could lose one million species. By the middle of the next century a quarter of all species may be lost.[3] This is less directly relevant to human life and human survival, but for this very reason it raises the difficult question of how much value we can and should give to non-human forms of life, whether or not they directly benefit us. That is a question I will want to return to. In fact of course we gain a great deal from a vast range of life forms, and we are gaining more and learning more of the benefits we could still gain. Even now we know relatively little about the earth, even less about those genetically rich areas in the tropical forest which contain over half the world's species of all forms of life. But we can be sure that in destroying these forests we are destroying vast resources that, if they had survived, might have turned out to be invaluable.

These problems are very different in kind and they obviously have to be dealt with in appropriately different ways, with special attention to the ecological and economic conditions of each region. There is no one global solution to ecological troubles (a point emphasized by the World Commission on Environment and Development).[4] But it should be clear already that these very different concerns touch each other at a number of points, and that each in its own way raises deeper questions about our modern way of life which affect the whole range of issues in our relations with the earth. The major point in common is that each area of crisis signifies a particular failure to integrate the modern industrial system with the given ecological system of the earth. The pollution of the earth is literally an elemental clash between two sets of incompatibles.[5] The erosion of the soil is the destruction of delicate sub-systems of the earth as a result of the over-expansion of modern agro-business; even in the South the loss of soil to the expanding deserts can be traced to the usurpation of fertile peasant land for cash-crops for the gobal economy, forcing the peasants on to poorer land. The depletion of natural non-renewable resources without obvious substitutes marks the striking incongruence between the ecological limits of the earth and the limitless ambition of the modern civilization. The annihilation of species highlights the incongruence between the self-renewing economy of the earth, for which waste does not exist, and the over-wasteful and destructive character of our industrial exploitation of the earth.

Not every ecological problem is to be laid at the door of modern industrialism. There were many ecological disasters in the world before the onset of the modern era.[6] But in surveying the areas of greatest concern today we cannot avoid the conclusion that they derive from the impact of industrial processes which are unsympathetic to the processes of nature. This has been observed from the very beginning of the industrialization process, when smoke and other industrial waste blighted the land and the people who had to live and work there. In those early stages, however, industrialists felt they could ignore these ecological costs because the natural ecology was able in the long term to absorb them. Industrialists today can no longer argue in this way, although many of them, understandably, still try. The industrial enterprise has expanded to the extent that indispensable resources are being used up, delicate ecological balances are being upset, and irreparable damage is being done to the life-system on which our own life depends. In a way directly parallel to the expansions of the modern economy and the modern security systems, the expansion of modern industrialism is meeting its limits. The importance of the historical moment was emphasized in the conclusion of the recent report of the World Commission on Environment and Development, *Our Common Future*:

> Over the course of this century, the relationship between the human world and the planet that sustains it has undergone a profound change. When the century began, neither human numbers nor technology had the power to

45

radically alter planetary systems. As the century closes, not only do vastly increased numbers and their activities have that power, but major, unintended changes are occurring in the atmosphere, in soils, in waters, among plants and animals, and in the relationships among all of these. The rate of change is outstripping the ability of scientific disciplines and our current capabilities to assess and advise. It is frustrating the attempts of political and economic institutions, which evolved in a different, more fragmented world, to adapt and cope.[7]

In its crudest form then the ecological crisis consists in the fact that the world has become top-heavy. The human world now dominates the natural world – at least in the narrow sense of the earth's biosphere – as a result of its phenomenal recent growth in size and power. Because of this domination, and of the ways in which it is maintained, we are threatening the structure of the natural world and therefore the structure of our human world as well.

But it would be misleading, I think, to suggest that the resolution of the crisis would be simply to reduce our impact on the earth, important though this obviously is. There is certainly a 'management problem' here: we need to quantify our resources more thoroughly, cost the processes of production and exchange, and introduce constraints into our use of resources to ensure that we have enough for future needs. But there is a deeper problem as well. It has to do with the industrial process itself, which seems to have a momentum of its own which defies any 'managerial' attempt to contain its expansive power. It is, as we have seen, constructed on the imperative to maximize the material output and to minimize the material cost. This is most obviously the case in the free-market economy of the West where, as we have seen, manufacturing is constrained by the demands of competition and short-term profit. But it is also the case in the centrally controlled economies of the East where the demand to increase production is imposed by government as a political and economic priority. As a consequence production is valued in terms of its quantifiable result, specifically, the value the commodity can acquire in economic exchange, whether on the open or the controlled market. This means that the whole production process is valued objectively in terms of the money it creates; or more simply that the industrial process is designed first of all to make money.

We have seen already how the logic of this process excludes the human costs entailed except in so far as they may limit the capacity for production. We should also notice here how the same logic excludes the ecological costs. From the viewpoint of modern industry the earth simply provides the resources or raw materials for production and a vast waste-disposal unit for its excrement. If resources are used up or waste-disposal areas polluted the earth can always, it is assumed, provide more of the same. The earth is therefore understood and treated in the same quantifiable terms by which we understand our industry. Land, forests, lakes, seas can all be given a price. We project on to the natural world the limited values of our own humanly constructed world.

This is the beginning of our modern estrangement from nature. It is exacerbated by the development of science as a means for the exploitation of nature. This is a sadly ironical development since science has also been such a powerful liberator of human minds, and has helped as much as any other form of knowledge to alert us to the dangers of our present crisis. Yet it cannot be denied that science has contributed to the crisis by allowing itself to be taken over by the interests of industrial development. For the larger part of modern science can be understood as the systematic analysis of matter in quantifiable terms, in terms, that is, which enable us to manipulate it for our own industrial purposes. The industrial pay-off of modern science is the one sure fact which persuades governments to invest so much money in it. But it also ensures that science is biased towards the exploitation of nature rather than towards a sympathetic appreciation of it. As a result we have become very good at extracting material from the earth, constructing new materials and material relations, and interfering with the earth's processes to make them serve our ends; but we are very poor at recognizing, let alone understanding, the implications of this interference for the earth itself.[8] We hardly have the intellectual resources even to begin. For the earth is not organized on the same principles on which we humans organize ourselves or our machines.

Expansion

If this were not enough, industrial expansion has stimulated other forms of expansion which have in turn stimulated the industrial process even more. The first of these, and perhaps the simplest and most basic, is the sheer growth of the human population. For centuries, and indeed millennia, growth has been relatively slow. At the time of the birth of Christ the population was about 250 million. It took sixteen centuries for that figure to double. During that time however the potential for growth was held down by a relatively short life expectancy: the vulnerability of human beings, especially in childhood, to disease, epidemics, shortages of food and violent struggles for land. With the improvement of agricultural production and conditions of health at the time of the industrial revolution in Europe, from the eighteenth century onwards, the population began to increase very rapidly. In addition to this there was, and is – given the survival of more children into adulthood – an inevitable acceleration in growth by sheer multiplication. If couples produce an average four children who survive, they in turn will produce eight in the next generation. It is this simple mathematical process that accounts for the fact that a one per cent rate of increase will double a population in seventy years, a two per cent increase in thirty-five years, a three per cent increase in only twenty-three years.[9] Each time, as the reproductive base gets wider, the increase of numbers accelerates. In this way we can plot the growth of population on a graph as an upward curve, which, if we project it into the future, suggests the phenomenonal increase of numbers we have still to expect. The world population was:

5 million in prehistoric times
250 million at the birth of Christ
500 million in 1650
1000 million in 1850
3500 million in 1970
5000 million today, and will be a projected
6000 million in 2000.

There is, however, a new limiting factor to growth which had led some ecologists to question the alarm suggested by these figures. It is pointed out that exponential growth has been made possible by improvements in agricultural and industrial production, but that these same factors also tend to reduce growth because in industrial society children become more of a liability than a resource and that therefore parents tend to have smaller families. As Barry Commoner puts it, 'Although population growth is an inherent feature of the progressive development of productive activities, it tends to be limited by the same force that stimulates it – the accumulation of social wealth and resources.'[10] We can notice this limiting effect in the obvious reduction in the rate of growth in the major industrial countries, although growth still continues – at between a half and one per cent. Instead of a simple upward curve, demographers are now talking about an 'S curve', suggesting that the world population will eventually level off sometime in the next century. They include within their calculation the actions that governments will inevitably have to take, sooner or later, to keep the numbers down. Partly because of this political uncertainty, estimates differ as to when and at what figure the world population will stabilize, ranging between 7.7 billion by the year 2060 and 14.2 billion by the year 2100.[11]

While the human population is now capable – because it has made itself capable – of growth by multiplication, the natural resources on which it depends remain relatively stable. (If the population of non-human species grows too rapidly it is brought down again by the ecological imbalance this creates, the same principle that had kept the human population stable in the past.) This is bound to lead to ecological stress as humans themselves compete for diminishing resources and as the resources themselves are either used up or made incapable of renewal.

In addition to this fundamental growth of numbers, and so to speak riding on top of it, is the growth of production and consumption. This has been spurred, significantly enough, by the pressure on resources we have just referred to. To cope with growing numbers it has been necessary to find ways of producing more goods from the same fund of resources, and where possible to find new usable resources as well. Agriculture has been made more productive by mechanization and the chemical control of fertility. Manufacture similarly has multiplied its output, and also made use of entirely new mineral resources. At the same time this 'development process', which we discussed in chapter 2, has acquired a dynamic of its own, ensuring an increase of production and exchange beyond the immediate demands of a growing population. The result has also been exponential; despite the ups and downs of the global economy there has been an overall increase in productivity during the last few hundred years, culminating in the very rapid growth of the last forty years. In 1950 the world manufactured only one-seventh of the goods it does today, and produced only one-third of the minerals. The following twenty-three years saw the most rapid industrial growth, with an average of seven per cent a year in manufacturing and five per cent a year in mining. Since then growth rates have slowed, but they have still been running at an average of three per cent.[12]

There is a third form of expansion, which, again, has ridden on the back of the one before, but also had a reciprocal effect. This is the technology explosion.[13] Science has been combined with technological invention in order to make goods more competitive in the global economy. The immense pressure on local industrial economies to keep pace with global expansion has led to an astonishing creativity in technological production. Much of this is humanly beneficial and ecologically benign. The development of micro-technology, for example, has greatly facilitated communications. But much of it involves the invention and construction of fundamentally new materials which are not to be found in nature and which – it becomes increasingly obvious – will not integrate with nature. The most obvious culprits here are the carbon compounds which are used in the creation of energy, and which are now being linked with such ecological disasters as the greenhouse effect and acid rain. The most obviously dangerous, however, is the technology of nuclear fire which draws on a primal power of the universe which is also capable of destroying it. The impact of this new technology on the earth is therefore of a different order from that of the older industrial exploitation, but it is evident that the one process affects the other and stimulates its further expansion.

All this suggests that there is a profound problem with the modern industrial process itself: that it is inherently expansive and aggressive in relation to nature, and that nothing short of a profound change of its character will avert the greatest ecological disaster. This is the burden of a British report written in 1972, *Blueprint for Survival*, but which in its time was thought by most people to be too radical and alarmist to be taken seriously. It said:

> The principle defect of the industrial way of life with its ethos of expansion is that it is not sustainable. Its termination within the lifetime of someone born today is inevitable – unless it continues to be sustained for a while longer by an entrenched minority at the cost of imposing great suffering on the rest of mankind. We can be certain, however, that sooner or later it will end (only the precise time and circumstance are in doubt) ... Radical change is both necessary and inevitable because the present increase in human numbers and *per capita* consumption, by disrupting ecosystems and depleting resources, are undermining the very foundations of survival.[14]

Estrangement

What I have been attempting to describe here is what we might call the objective character of the present crisis. I have suggested that, objectively, the crisis consists in the damaging impact of the artificial world we have constructed for our material betterment on the natural world; or more precisely, in the strained and one-sided relationship between our industrial system and the global ecosystem which it exploits and on which it finally depends. But the crisis goes deeper than this, because the industrial system which is doing the damage is something we have come to depend on and to which indeed we are for the most part strongly committed. The crisis has a subjective side to it which makes it rather more difficult to come to terms with.

On a practical level there is the fact that, unless we belong to the relatively small number of tribal people or traditional villagers, we could not survive without the grace of the modern industrial system. We would lack the skills, resources and social organization to live independently. If large numbers of us nevertheless tried to recover those pre-industrial skills and to reorganize ourselves appropriately for a life on the land, we should find that there were now far too many people in the world for the amount of land that was available.

What is true of individuals is also, in another way, true of collectivities. Nations which have once committed themselves to modernization cannot switch back to the older traditions, nor easily switch over to some newer form of independence. The experiences of the Ujamaa project in Tanzania and the Kibbutz movement in Israel bear witness to the severe pressures that any such bid for economic self-sufficiency must suffer. It may be the case that, objectively, the future has to lie with experimentation of this kind, but subjectively it is difficult to achieve because we are already in every aspect of our lives enmeshed in modernity. And for collectivities as much as for individuals the modern system of producing life's necessities brings with it all the other trappings of modernity which make that system workable and livable. It brings, inevitably, modern science and technology, telecommunications, bureaucratization of business and government, nationalism, representative government under the name of democracy, state control of education (which is in turn geared to the rationalization of modernity) and the repression or marginalization of traditional culture, especially religion. Modernity in this sense is the new cultural empire of the world.[15] There is very little space, objectively or subjectively, that lies beyond its power.

As modernity increases its power we become increasingly more dependent on it. Through new forms of advertising, communication and entertainment it is able to reach into our minds more effectively than any great preachers or prelates of the past. We can be sold what we thought we didn't need, persuaded to seek our satisfaction in commodities that can be bought, persuaded indeed that consuming is itself the greatest source of pleasure. We can learn to live our lives vicariously through the fantasies of TV soap operas, sports programmes and 'family games'. Little by little it wins over our commitment and devotion.

In such ways we imbibe the values of the process on which our lives depend, or rather on which we perceive our lives to depend. We internalize the industrial system in, e.g., making a personal goal of money and in perceiving our own 'success' as individuals or families in terms of material expansion. This attitude proves in turn to be important for the global industrial process, because it enables it to expand beyond the immediate or basic needs of those for whom it provides. By stimulating a personal ethos of 'more means better', the industrial process can continue to grow almost indefinitely.

We may recognize, of course, that in order to survive our industrial system needs to stimulate demand even when this means creating 'needs' where none existed before, but this may not help us very much in detaching ourselves emotionally and spiritually. And we cannot so easily get rid of substitute needs when we have lost some of the immediate satisfactions which they have replaced. We no longer have access to ordinary community life, to a natural and joyous relationship with nature. We no longer have the kind of immediate satisfactions of work which we might have had in the past. It is not only our industrial system that is alien to nature. We ourselves, through our participation in industrial society, have also become alienated from nature, to some extent also from our own natural bodies. In the somewhat unreal world of our own making we have to seek substitute satisfactions through consumerism, where buying becomes the ritual through which the sacrament of meaning and goodness is made available to us.

It would seem to follow from this that there is something like a religion embedded in our commitment to growth and modern industrial progress. For if it is true that we are committed to these values to the extent that we cannot live without them we would have to conclude that they have become, from a subjective point of view, ultimate and absolute, that in a peculiarly modern sense they have become our gods.

We have seen something of the tacit religion of modernity in our reflection on the modern pursuit of wealth and security. We then identified the idols of this religion, following a cue from Francis Bacon, as those of the weapon, the tribe and the market place. In our reflection here it is becoming clear that our attachment to these idols is formed in the systematic organization of our modern way of life, which revolves around the specifically modern process of producing, selling and consuming the basic necessities of life. It transforms work into the task of making money, personal fulfillment into individual success, security into the possession of wealth, satisfaction of need into the consumption of goods, and quest for meaning in life into the pursuit of status and power. But in our commitment to this way of life we have also sacrificed much. We have created a safe, artificial world of our own, designed to meet every possible need, but in doing so we have become estranged from our original life with one another and with nature. Experiences of love, beauty, adventure, awe, sensuousness have to be mediated, as in a traditional act of worship, through manufactured objects. But our profound belief in those objects has made us insensitive to the damage they are doing to that alienated world of nature on which in fact our lives primarily depend. We are therefore estranged from the very reality with which we need to achieve a close relationship. This makes our crisis a spiritual one.

Reconciliation

Yet once again we can find within the crisis the seeds of its own solution. We may be filled with despair at what appears to be an inevitable outcome, but we can also find in the experience of despair some new grounds for hope. This is because, as with the nuclear crisis, the implied threat touches the motivations that sustain it. For one thing, our confident assumption that we depend primarily on ourselves and our technology is shown to be nothing short of an illusion. It might appear, from the view point of life in the cities, that we have created our own environment and no longer need the one provided by nature. We may convince ourselves that whereas primitive people depended on nature in every aspect of their lives we have managed to find alternatives to nature in the products of our own technological ingenuity. And it is true, of course, that most of us live our lives at a great distance from nature and rarely experience it in the raw. But whatever our immediate and obvious dependencies may be, we are now forced to recognize that we are all finally sons and daughters of the earth, and that the cities and technologies we have so proudly constructed for ourselves are entirely derived from the earth's own riches. The air we breathe, the food we eat, the material of our houses and our many possessions, even the latest gadgets of micro-technology are all from nature and depend on nature's resourcefulness for their continuing availability. Also, the secular religion which led us to believe that we were heading for an earthly paradise is now shown by the threat of ecological breakdown to be a fundamentally false religion. However, with the exposure of our collective falsehoods there comes also a revelation of a deeper truth by which we could live and which would give us a basis for a genuine hope for the future. In being shown that we as human beings are not fundamentally apart from nature or alien to it, we are shown that we are part of a whole, that we belong together, that we live in and with and through each other.

This is evident from the way in which ecological damage is done and new threats occur. Abuse of one part of the environment will lead to abuse elsewhere, and possibly, eventually, to abuse of human life. In our use of the earth we may work on the assumption that the process is linear, at one end the endless resources of nature and at the other end its bottomless pit for industrial waste. In fact the process is always circular. Whether creatively or destructively we are always part of the circle.[16]

The new science of ecology has done a great deal to illuminate this situation, demonstrating, among other things, how science is capable of other developments than those of industrial exploitation. Avoiding the fragmentation and reductionism of so much modern science it tries to understand living things in relation to one another. It is therefore a study of environments, of totalities, and on the largest scale, of the totality of life on earth. It is 'the science of planetary housekeeping', says Commoner, playing on the original Greek meaning of eco (*oikos*, house). 'For the environment is, so to speak, the house created on the earth *by* living things *for* living things.' One of the most valuable finds of ecology in fact is the discovery of global integration and mutual support within the ecosystem, modifying the impression of evolutionary theory that everything competes with everything else. But Commoner adds, conceding the difficulty of this study:

> Understanding the ecosphere comes hard because, to the modern mind, it is a curiously foreign place. We have become accustomed to think of separate, singular events, each dependent upon a unique, singular cause. But in the ecosphere every effect is also a cause: an animal's waste becomes food for soil bacteria; what bacteria excrete nourishes plants; animals eat the plants. Such ecological cycles are hard to fit into human experience in the age of

technology, where machine A always yields product B, and product B, once used, is cast away, having no further meaning for the machine, the product, or the user.[17]

According to some ecologists the theoretical task involved in grasping these cycles and totalities of nature is nothing short of a 'paradigm shift'.[18] One of the most impressive models used in this venture is the cybernetic model derived from the study and use of computers. It has the advantage of being able to demonstrate *inter*dependencies between all elements involved instead of one-way causations. However, there is, I believe, a serious danger in supposing that even the best scientific model can comprise the totality of our world. Ecology works as a science when, with other sciences, it selects an object of study – however large or abstract – which is open to objective investigation. Ecology is therefore limited because it excludes, necessarily, our full human involvement in the various processes it examines. To gain a sense of our own interaction with the planet, a sense of our unity as human beings with all other living things, we need a mode of thinking which can include the thinker as well as the thought about, the subject as well as the object.

Moreover the truth being revealed to us in the ecological crisis is not only a scientific truth, but a wider truth of our collective, historical experience. It is a truth which concerns both facts of our situation and our own unique human experience of the situation, and therefore of course our special responsibility towards it. It is as much about us as it is about the world out there, and so to grasp that truth intellectually we need to recognize ourselves in it and become more fully aware of ourselves as actors and observers in the world. If we recognize our interconnectedness only in a general or abstract way – in terms of 'cells of energy' or 'webs of life' e.g. – we shall not be helped to *feel* differently about nature and therefore act differently towards it.

There is also the fact, which we have discussed at some length, that our human relation to the earth does not exemplify the ecological integration we can witness elsewhere. As a species we no longer fit into the overall pattern. We might even be described as a cancerous growth on the global ecosystem, since we draw our life from it in such a way as to drain it of life. As the philosopher Nietzsche said, 'spirit is life which itself cuts into life'. Despite our fundamental unity with nature there is obviously also a conflict.

How are we to approach this problem? How do we make sense of the unity of life without ignoring the unique situation of human beings as free and estranged, who are both part of nature but also distinct from it in a way that cannot be fully grasped scientifically? We find a clue to this, I think, in our relationship with other human beings. In our life with fellow human beings we can recognize a fundamental dilemma. On the one hand we are mutually dependent and need for our own sakes to co-operate sensitively with one another. On the other hand we are basically anxious for ourselves, and are prepared to sacrifice the interests of others to our own if there seems to be a conflict between them. We tend in fact to regard other people as a means to our own betterment, and to seek co-operation with them only if we can see an immediate benefit to ourselves in so doing. But time and again such short-sightedness lets us down. We get into quarrels, feel lonely and isolated, are threatened by others and perhaps by life itself. Out of such painful experiences however there may come a deeper insight which persuades us to cherish others more for their own sake, to find our fulfillment as individuals in giving ourselves generously to others and working for harmonious relations. As a result we experience other people differently. They are no longer objects of fear against whom we have to defend ourselves, by e.g. keeping our distance, playing our cards tight to the chest, finding ways to control the situation. They are more recognizable as people like ourselves who respond to warmth and honesty. We find that, paradoxical as it may at first seem, we gain a sense of security with others, or certain others at least, when we are open with them, direct, natural and spontaneous. Such of course is the nature of good friendship.

One important feature of good friendship, as with intense love relations, is that we lose our feeling of isolation and alienation. There is an experience of human unity and then a sense of belonging. In larger groups too we can experience the same self-transcending unity with other people, although we have to recognize that such experience can also be distorted or manipulated, or fabricated indeed, as when, e.g. a charismatic leader stirs up mass feeling at a religious or political rally. In cases of genuine self-transcendence unity is not given as a fact of life, it is arrived at through struggle and commitment. And once arrived at it cannot then be taken for granted. It must be guarded with our love.

Our situation with other living beings is very similar, I would suggest. On the one hand we have a fundamental unity with life on earth in the sense that we are mutually dependent and inescapably part of the global ecosystem. On the other hand, because of our unique situation as human beings – with freedom of choice, anxiety for ourselves and increasing physical power – we can all too easily act against the interests of life as a whole and thus in the long term against our own human interests. Whether we are pessimistic or not about the tendency of humans to act destructively we cannot deny that when they do they do so (most of them) as a matter of choice, and that when they suffer as a result they are generally capable of learning to do otherwise. (An important exception to this rule concerns the many people in the South who are forced to destroy their environment, and therefore their long term security, in order to stay alive in the short term. The loss of freedom to act is part of their poverty.) There does also seem to be a rather fundamental choice here, as with our relations with fellow human beings: either we choose to regard life as a direct means to our own good, or we cherish it for its own sake. We either calculate and manipulate, keeping ourselves at a distance, or we identify and feel and care. We are of course too familiar with the first attitude; our approach to life on earth is predominantly exploitative and manipulative, since we suppose it exists for our benefit. The other attitude is therefore rarely expressed, in public at least, since in private we may care greatly for living beings.

Because of the cultural estrangement from nature, which I discussed before, it is perhaps not surprising that we are so insensitive to it. But the situation is serious enough to demand that we learn sensitivity. There are clearly limits to treating nature as so many 'things' at our disposal. What seems to be required of us here, as with our strained relations with the people of the planet, is that we learn to make friends with nature.

The Jewish philosopher Martin Buber has a remarkable

passage in his book *I and Thou* in which he describes the different possible ways of relating to a tree. It is intended as an illustration of different ways of relating to nature.

I contemplate a tree.

I can accept it as a picture: a rigid pillar in a flood of light, or splashes of green traversed by the gentleness of the blue silver ground ... I can assign it to a species and observe it as an instance, with an eye to its construction and its way of life.

I can overcome its uniqueness and form so rigorously that I recognize it only as an expression of the law – those laws according to which a constant opposition of forces is continually adjusted, or those laws according to which the elements mix and separate.

I can dissolve it into a number, into a pure relation between numbers, and eternalize it. Throughout all of this the tree remains my object and has its place and its time span, its kind and condition.

But it can also happen, if will and grace are joined, that as I contemplate the tree I am drawn into a relation, and the tree ceases to be an It ...

This does not require me to forego any of the modes of contemplation. There is nothing that I must not see in order to see, and there is no knowledge that I must forget. Rather is everything, picture and movement, species and instance, law and number included and inseparably fused ...

The tree is no impression, no play of my imagination, no aspect of a mood; it confronts me bodily and has to deal with me as I must deal with it – only differently.

One should not try to dilute the meaning of the relation: relation is reciprocity.[19]

Unity with life in this case is not given as a fact of nature. As in our relations with humans it arises as we positively affirm life. Unity is a possibility which is there for us to realize, through our contemplation, sensitivity and care.

Is the same possibility open in relation to the earth as a whole? It was envisaged by the philosopher William James who said 'The universe is no longer a mere "It" to us, but a "Thou" if we are religious.'[20] This was certainly a possibility for contemplation. For us, not so many years later, there is a very concrete possibility, indeed exigency, in relation to the earth in particular. While contemplating its unity mystically or ecologically we can also be alarmed at its possible disintegration, unless we positively take care of it. In that contemplation of loss, or possible loss, the earth can assume a unique and startling value for us. (Is it a mere coincidence that the first photograph of the earth should have appeared at the time when its life was first threatened? It is in any case a powerful image of what we now feel.) As the theologian Dorothée Sölle has said,

> The earth is sacred. Ten years ago I was not so conscious of the sacredness of the earth. It is when we are confronted with the utter threat to that which we love that we rediscover the wellsprings of our love.[21]

The mystic writer Thich Nhat Han has urged that we include this experience in our contemplation, so as 'to hear within ourselves the sounds of the earth crying'. Was the early Christian Paul doing just this when he envisaged the creation as a woman in labour? She 'groans' and 'waits for the glorious liberty of the children of God' (Rom. 8.22f.), that is, we must suppose, for the creation of a new heaven and new earth.[22] Francis of Assisi, according to his early biographer, echoing the passage from Paul, 'discerned the hidden things of creation with the eye of the heart, as one who had already escaped into the glorious liberty of the children of God'.[23]

Before leaping into postures of responsibility and 'stewardship', or determining hastily to 'take control of the situation', we need to gain a sense of the earth as a living whole within which and on which we live our daily lives, both individually and together, and to feel within ourselves the pain of its distress.

But out of the wonder and out of the anguish there may come a new love. And in the affirmation of the earth in love, addressing the earth as 'you' with all our being, we may find unity with the earth. The Buddhist may find a compassion for the earth not unlike his or her compassion for suffering human beings. The Christian or the Jew or the Muslim may find a 'love for the neighbour' which up till then had been confined to human neighbours. But the earth no less than humans, our tradition tells us, was created by God for the glory of God – and God, having created it, declared that it was 'very good' (Gen. 1.31).

The symbol of that first natural environment for humans was a garden.

> The Lord God formed man of dust from the ground, and breathed into his nostrils the breath of life; and man became a living being. And the Lord God planted a garden in Eden, in the east; and there he put the man whom he had formed. And out of the ground the Lord God made to grow every tree that is pleasant to the sight and good for food, the tree of life also in the midst of the garden, and the tree of the knowledge of good and evil ... The Lord God took the man and put him in the garden of Eden to till it and keep it (Gen. 2.7–15).

But the man and his wife were banished from the garden because they had insisted on knowing and doing things for themselves.

> Then the Lord God said, 'Behold, the man has become like one of us, knowing good and evil; and now, lest he put forth his hand and take also of the tree of life, and eat, and live forever' – therefore the Lord God sent him forth from the garden of Eden, to till the ground from which he was taken. He drove out the man; and at the east of the garden of Eden he placed the cherubim, and a flaming sword which turned every way, to guard the way to the tree of life (Gen. 3.22–24).

That garden was also to be a symbol of 'paradise regained', when, as the prophet Isaiah put it, God would 'create a new heaven and a new earth, and the former things shall not be remembered' (Isa. 65.17). The Christian writer of the Book of Revelation picks up that theme, blending it with the more familiar hope of a new city:

> And he who sat upon the throne said, 'Behold, I make all things new' ... Then he showed me the river of the water of life, bright as crystal, flowing from the throne of God and the Lamb through the middle of the street of the city; also, on either side of the river, the tree of life with its twelve kinds of fruit ... (Rev. 21.5; 22.1f.).

For us the symbols of paradise and kingdom of God must merge. To befriend the earth we must first let go the idolatries that pervade our modern world. But also, to care for one another economically and politically, which is an imperative of the kingdom, we must also care for the earth which is our first and last resource. If the kingdom of God means, in our global situation, that people of all nations and classes be regarded as one community, the hope of paradise means that all living creatures are now included in that community.

We have already considered the thought – in relation to other major issues – that our sense of identity has to be as wide as the range of the relationships we have to live with. We cannot survive politically unless we identify ourselves with something larger than our individual nations or even power blocs: our security in facing possible threats from outside has to be a 'common security'. Similarly in economic relations we have to see ourselves as rich people of the North in community with the poor people of the South, otherwise our own economy may break down. Our sense of identity has to become wider and wider. In our ecological situation, however, we can see that it has to go wider still, to include not only all the people of the earth, but also all living creatures, indeed the earth itself. We now belong to the community of the earth. It is in this community, we have to say, and only in this community, that we shall be able to live as humans with a future to hope for and work for.

One implication of this new development is that we humans will have to drop our almost natural sense of superiority in relation to other species. No doubt in the past, in the distant past, we needed a strong sense of our value in order to survive in a world where, so to speak, we were greatly outnumbered. This is reflected in the biblical story which describes the creation of humans 'in the image and likeness' of God. In our time it is just as important to see something of God in every other creature God has made, without at the same time denying what is special to our own human race. This is the corollary of the view that we derive our being and life from the earth but that we are also able, if we choose, to destroy it. This balance in our relationship, closer now to our relationship with fellow human beings, gives other creatures a very special significance for us. If we can call human life sacred – because we recognize how much our own life is bound up with others, how much our life derives meaning and value from theirs – we can, and surely must, call all life sacred.

This is not to say that the earth is divine, which would imply that it was the ultimate source of our life. The earth cannot be ultimate precisely because it is fragile and vulnerable. If the earth was once a goddess we humans have become gods and goddesses too. We have acquired the global power to preserve or to destroy. We cannot regress now to an attitude of simple dependency. This is an important point since there are many people in the ecological movement who have abandoned both Christianity and secularism in favour of an ecologically sensitive paganism. The move is under-standable, but it is also, we might say, historically insensitive. That is, it fails to recognize the historical newness of our situation, in which, to quote the Bruntland Report again, 'the relationship between the human world and the planet that sustains it has undergone a profound change'.[24] Since our future depends on our caring for the earth we must do nothing which obscures our new responsibility. If we see the earth as sacred we must recognize the sacred in ourselves as well. If we think of the earth as mother we must recognize ourselves as children who have now grown up.[25] If in our arrogant adulthood we have hurt mother earth we can, instead of simply admitting to our faults, seek a genuine and mature reconciliation.

Nevertheless, it may still be important to relate to what *is* ultimate, especially if the crisis evokes in us a disturbing insecurity. Perhaps we can discover through the delicate interdependence of life on earth the deepest source of life which gives unity and meaning to all life. Its very finitude – its limitedness, fragility, transience – leads us to find some-thing beyond it which is reliable, invulnerable. This can only be the infinite. But the infinite is not something we can grasp or possess, even intellectually. It can be known and trusted, in Buber's language, only as 'you', the 'eternal you' we can dimly sense in every encounter with an earthly 'you'. It is inevitably elusive, and our experience of it must also be fragile and transient, but it may be enough to give us the basic confidence in life that we need, at least enough to wean us off the depen-dence on 'things' which has made them into damaging idols.

FIVE

Conclusion

The recognition of a tacit religion within modernity has a number of important implications both for our understanding of religion in the global situation and for our practical response to the situation. It relieves us from simplistic moralizing, e.g. the argument that world poverty or environmental damage is due simply to 'greed' and that therefore the solution to these problems is for those concerned to restrain their appetites and allow others to have their share. There is sufficient truth in this argument, of course, to encourage us to give it a second thought. But it is too naive and too individualistic to count as an analysis of the present situation. For this we have to look more carefully at the nature of our attachment to material progress. The value of a theological analysis, such as we have been looking for here, is that it enables us to relate people's behaviour to what they take to be the ultimate or final reality; and then to relate that understanding of reality to the basic needs and concerns of their lives. None of this precludes psychological or economic analyses, which have in fact been drawn on in the course of this discussion. But, as I argued at the beginning, theology has its own special interest in relating everything in human life, as far as possible, to its ultimate source and context.

Security and identity

In relation to the present global crisis the most illuminating category for theological analysis seems to be the old prophetic concept of idolatry. As a general theological category it has been refined somewhat from its original use in relation to the religions of the ancient world, where 'images' – the original meaning of idols – were often regarded as embodiments of divine or saving reality. The first critique of idols in ancient Israel, however, went beyond the rejection of physical representations of God – which has remained its popular meaning – to a criticism of the fundamental human attitude which required such representations. We saw this in relation to the prophet Isaiah in chapter 2, where the prophet openly mocks the worshipper of idols for submitting himself totally to an object he himself has made.

> All who make idols are nothing, and the things they delight in do not profit ... He makes a god and worships it, he makes it a graven image, and falls down before it ... Half of it he burns in the fire ... and the rest of it he makes into a god, his idol ... They do not know, nor do they discern ... He feeds on ashes: a deluded man has led him astray and he cannot deliver himself or say 'Is there not a lie in my right hand?' (Isa. 44.9–20).

The real fault of idolatry is not in the mistake of thinking that God can be made visible or tangible, serious though that is, but in treating God exactly as we would treat things, as if God existed for our benefit and could be used at any time to satisfy our needs.

But why should anyone be so stupid as to suppose that the ultimate basis of their existence could be identified with an object that they themselves have made? This of course is also the uncomfortable question we have to ask ourselves as we recognize that our dependence on and belief in the production of 'things' amounts to a modern version of idolatry. To answer this we would have to consider the kind of need that idolatry is meeting. To the worshipper of course the idol is far more than the mere object that the rest of us can see and touch. It is invested with power, life, profound significance. That is precisely its divine reality. It therefore answers a need which has little to do with material want, but everything to do with a sense of insecurity in the world and a fear that life will simply not make sense. These are fairly universal feelings, and may well be rooted in the universal human experience of self-awareness: the awareness that we are subject to forces beyond our understanding and control, that the suffering we experience as a result of this has no inherent rhyme or reason, and that each of us is ultimately alone in the world, most notably at the point of our own death. In the light of this it seems not wholly unreasonable to look for something outside us that will provide the reality we lack. Nor does it seem unreasonable to look for something fairly tangible or imaginable, for otherwise there is nothing to hold on to. To insist, on the basis of a greater insight, that nothing tangible could ever be the source of meaning and value would be simply to deny the one source available.

There is an interesting passage in the New Testament where Paul condemns idolatry but suggests at the same time that it might be rooted in the fear of the alternative.

> For the wrath of God is revealed from heaven against all ungodliness and wickedness of men who by their wickedness suppress the truth. For what can be known about God is plain to them, because God has shown it to them. Ever since the creation of the world his invisible nature, namely, his eternal power and deity, has been clearly perceived in the things that have been made. So they are without excuse; for although they knew God they did not honour him as God or give thanks to him, but they became futile in their thinking and their senseless minds were darkened. Claiming to be wise they became fools, and exchanged the glory of the immortal God for images resembling mortal man or birds or animals or reptiles ... They exchanged the truth about God for a lie and worshipped and served the creature rather than the Creator, who is blessed for ever! Amen (Rom. 1.18–25).

Paul seems to be suggesting here that idolatry is a response to the disclosure of 'the eternal power' of God through 'the things that have been made', but which actually proved to be too much, too overwhelming. Confronted with this awesome infinity – the mysterious and impenetrable origin of everything – people become anxious and turn to something tangible, something they can obviously trust and appeal to. They turn to 'the creature rather than the Creator'. It is futile, obviously, because nothing that is 'made' can sustain the absolute trust that is placed in it, but emotionally and existentially it is at least understandable.

The historic project of modernity can be viewed in this light. Its historical roots no doubt lie in the anxieties awakened by poverty, plague and civil war in early modern Europe. Its dream, so well articulated by Francis Bacon, was in itself quite laudable: that human beings should begin to take responsibility for the situation in which they lived, and should struggle through the advancement of learning, technical skill and human organization to create the wealth that would make life bearable. But the implementation of this dream assumed a form that made its realization impossible. The pursuit of wealth and power became an end in itself. A responsible concern for the welfare of one's fellow human beings, as Bacon expressed it, was translated into an irresponsible and almost immature concern to accumulate wealth for oneself.

The elevation of a natural and proper concern (as one among many) to the status of an absolute is one way of defining idolatry.[1] It is not the pursuit of wealth or power as such which constitutes idolatry or leads to evil. Wealth and power after all are necessary conditions of human existence. They would need to be actively pursued along with other concerns which sustain our life, such as concern for the community and concern for meaning and knowledge. All human societies have therefore supported material values, alongside social and spiritual values. It is only when one value is emphasized to the exclusion of others that profound problems arise, and it then becomes tyrannical and destructive. Modern Western society seems to be unique in the history of the world in elevating material values to the point where they virtually exclude all others.

It has been argued in this book that the distinctly modern attempts to find security in the world are exposed as futile by the global process they have set in motion, inevitably leading to crisis. It is unlikely, however, that this historic, prophetic exposure will of itself lead to any fundamental change. As well as disclosing a new and profounder truth it may just as well heighten anxiety and drive people into ever more absurd and crass idolatries. Religious people may distort their faith into the most fanatical fundamentalism. Others may project their fears wholly on to tangible enemies who, as scapegoats, will be made to suffer for the evil they have supposedly brought on to the world.[2] Powerful individuals may make a cult of making money, wholly oblivious and apparently indifferent to the misery this may bring to other people. As with many cults of the past, when the prevailing religion fails to provide the security and significance people are looking for they are very likely to turn to a more extreme version of the same thing, or to an equally extreme version of something that came before.

Yet the crisis, as we have seen, does have a positive potentiality. With its exposure of pretensions and illusions it does hint at an alternative development: economically towards co-operation and fair trading, politically towards global community, and, most dramatically perhaps, ecologically towards an integration of life on earth. In each case I felt bold enough to describe this as revelation, consciously reverting to the old prophetic ideas that God speaks to us through historical situations. However, because of the crudity of so much talk of revelation and prophecy, I felt it necessary to emphasize that what is revealed to us in the emerging situation has nothing to do with plans or predetermined scenarios. It has to do with new possibilities which are open for us to realize. The situation calls for responsibility, not infantile dependence. What the Hebrew prophets spoke about is indeed relevant to us: a new world is coming where justice and peace will prevail, but only if we seize the opportunity before us to bring it about.

The point has significance in another respect also. There is a scientific equivalent to the religious doctrine of divine plans which tells us that the earth is in fact, already, one single organism and that it is simply up to us to adapt to it. We have come across this idea already in relation to ecology, which is sometimes proposed as a model for human action and organization. The serious fault in this way of thinking, as we also noted, is that the ecological model, though suited to natural habitats, including of course the global habitat, cannot adequately include the activity and impact of human beings, with their distinctive freedoms. There is indeed in the ecological crisis a revelation of a new earth in which humans are reconciled not only with one another but also with the earth which for so long they have exploited. But again, it is a revelation of possibility; the integrity of life on this scale and with this depth of human commitment will be something new, achieved at a new and more sophisticated level of integration.[3] It is in a sense, to use another biblical phrase, a 'new creation' (II Cor. 5.17), and we ourselves would be involved in creating it. Of course, it would not and could not ignore the structural unities that already exist – the interdependence of all living things and the specific interdependence of human societies. These would have to be strongly affirmed as a necessary condition of achieving unity of a different order, as unity of freedom and mutual recognition.

I realize, however, that in emphasizing unity as a possibility rather than an actuality I am making this global project sound wholly unrealistic. At least with traditional Christian ideas of providence and predestination, as with Marx's historical determinism, the future could be guaranteed. But it has to be said that to expect a guarantee of this sort, if we are not to deny human freedom and responsibility altogether, is to ask for a security that cannot be had – another tangible security in place of the material idols we had supposedly left behind. If the future is genuinely open – that is, if humans are really free and responsible in their actions – and if all material things are subject to change and decay, then our security cannot lie in the persistence of things or the persistence of human institutions. It has to lie elsewhere, somewhere within the process of change and somehow within ourselves, so that it is not in the least threatened by knowing we are responsible. One way of locating this would be to say that it lies in the creative source of the whole changing reality, involving our own creative input, obviously, but also reaching beyond that to involve the whole of reality as we are aware of it. This is not something we can know in the ordinary sense, because it lies beyond the range of our senses and intellectual penetration. We can nonetheless be aware of it in a number of ways: as the limit of our understanding, where reality fades into nothingness, apparently to an infinity; as the infinite void that gives us our deepest insecurity when we think of the accident of our own existence, and its inevitable end; and as the mysterious reason for their being anything at all. These are dizzy thoughts that leave us unsettled. But we can also be aware of it more positively when we experience ourselves or others acting creatively and so participating in the creative process of the universe itself. As *objects* of the creative process we can feel futile and pointless, alienated and alone, pushed along by the apparently meaningless flow of events. As *subjects* of the process we can feel ourselves to be part of it, united with it, as we actively give meaning to its randomness and uncertainty. We noted this possibility in relation to the nuclear threat which confronts us with such a stark end to existence that the struggle to remove the threat and establish the conditions of survival becomes a creative affirmation of life. In this sense we can know or be aware of the creative source of our being and of all being.

It is still customary, even among scientists, to think of the creation of the world quite straightforwardly as an event in the past, the first, initiating event in the history of the universe. But the notion of a first event, which itself has no cause, no preceding event to explain it, must itself be unintelligible. The act of God 'creating' the world is therefore also unintelligible, for in order to make sense of this we would have to imagine a time before there was a world, which is impossible. But if instead we understand creation as the process by which things come to be we can make sense of it, because new things are happening all the time, new realities are coming into existence, and we human beings, with our earth, are evidently involved in the process. Part of the newness of our appearance as *homo sapiens* on the earth is the capacity to relate in many different ways to the earth and to ourselves, and also to choose between these different ways. It is therefore given to us to create something new, quite consciously and as an act of freedom. And within the range of our options we have what we might call a fundamental option, to choose life or to take it for granted, to affirm it or to deny it. But in choosing and affirming it we would be uniting with the creative source of life itself, and potentially at least, aware of so doing.

Although a sense of God does not assure us about any eventuality in the future, but contains within it an acceptance of risk, what is sometimes called a 'holy insecurity', it nevertheless encourages a trust in other human beings and the natural processes of life, which does in effect make us more secure. This is paradoxical no doubt, but an indisputable fact of experience. To understand this we have to recognize how placing confidence in God affects our relationship with others. To begin with it affects our perception of them as individuals or groups because we recognize in them the same creativity we have come to accept in ourselves, that is, the same potential for the creative affirmation of life and its unity. This may go clean against our previous conception of them, which may well have been influenced by our need to see them as fundamentally different from us, possibly inferior or superior, or plainly hostile. However, the recognition of a common, transcendent source of human life and of life in general leads to a different perception of human identity: to the extent that we can act on and live by that recognition we assume a new identity. To the extent that we can affirm other people in this relation to the transcendent we confer a new identity upon them. We can love our neighbours as *ourselves*. In the context of global tensions we can assume a global identity, accepting ourselves and therefore others too as members of the one community of life on earth, as against an exclusively individual or national identity. As people respond to one another out of this perception they confirm this perception in practice. What starts out as an affirmation becomes a reality: people enter into community across long-standing barriers and divides.

There is also a larger interhuman process here, for integration between people is not achieved by my or anyone's individual action. It is in the reciprocity of actions and their cumulative effect that change is brought about. Even then of course there may be setbacks and resistance. Faith in the transcendent therefore translates into hope.

What then is hoped for? Let me risk a description: an order of life in which each person is affirmed by the other, in which each *can* be affirmed and can affirm. It presupposes the freedom of all human beings to act and live from their own deepest insights, so that the bonds of human society can be formed of trust and mutual respect. It is not an order that can be imposed from above; on the contrary, all humanly constructed hierachies will be done away with. Similarly in relation to the earth humans will no longer see themselves as superior to other forms of life, but will respect all life of whatever form and care for the integrity of the earth as a condition of life for all of us.

71

The present significance of the historical Jesus

The picture of a possible world, made possible by a universal trust in the one transcendent source of our common life, seems to be identical with what Jesus had in mind with 'the kingdom of God'. This gives Jesus' life and teaching, which were singlemindedly devoted to the kingdom, a particular relevance to us. This is perhaps surprising since it has often been supposed either that Jesus had a wholly other-worldly picture in mind or that he expected a supernatural intervention into history within a very short time. It can then be inferred that Jesus is relevant only to those who can accept his other-worldly view or can think their way round his apparent mistake in expecting a sudden end to the world. But his teaching looks very different if we suppose that he was responding to a spiritual crisis in the world of his time and discerning in the crisis the possibility of a new world emerging which resembled what prophets and sages had promised in the past. The urgency and depth of our own world crisis might in fact help us to recover Jesus' insight into a situation that was not too dissimilar; it is usually the case, is it not, that we understand people best when we recognize in their words and actions a response to a situation similar to our own. In this we would be helped by some recent developments in biblical scholarship, although this is not the place to go into it in any detail.[4]

The crisis that Jesus faced in the world of his time seems to have focussed on the possibility of a war between Israel and Rome in which Israel would most certainly be destroyed. We cannot be absolutely sure about this because the records were compiled outside Israel at a much later time, when, for the followers of Jesus at any rate, the crisis was no longer real and Jesus had to be seen as still relevant in another time and place. But if we attempt to reconstruct the life of Jesus in the context of his own time and place we can get a reasonably convincing picture of what he was about; and it becomes reasonably certain that he was expecting a violent showdown with the imperial rulers and set out to warn people against it.[5] Our firmest piece of evidence for this is that, of all the religious and political groups he might have identified with, he chose to identify himself with John the Baptist, by accepting his baptism. John's distinctive message had been a warning to Israel to avoid the coming violence – which would only be God's judgment on them – by fundamentally changing their ways. Other religious groups predicted disaster and judgment for Israel's enemies, but not for Israel; none of them, not even the puritanical Essenes, called on Israel to repent. The assumption in John's message was that the crisis in relation to Israel's enemies was largely Israel's responsibility. If she had not sought wealth and power and prestige she would not be in confrontation with Rome. Her only salvation, therefore, was by way of repentence, of which John's baptism in the river was a public symbol.

Jesus did not apparently follow John for long, although he always spoke in awe of him, as 'the greatest born of woman'. He had a different mission, because he recognized in the crisis and its ominous threat the possibility of such a thorough-going and widespread change of heart in Israel that the kingdom of God itself would come. As compared with John his preaching was therefore good news. As the Gospel of Mark neatly summarizes it:

> After John was arrested, Jesus came into Galilee, preaching the good news of God, and saying, 'The time is fulfilled, and the kingdom of God is at hand; repent, and believe the good news (Mark 1.14, 15).

The success of his mission in Galilee obviously encouraged him to believe that a fundamental change was on the way and that disaster could be averted. Yet his preaching met with little response from Jews in positions of wealth and power. This is perhaps not surprising. His teaching on wealth and power was far too radical for their tastes: if taken seriously it would undermine their position in society. Yet such people were only a minority, albeit a dominant one. Most people seem to have welcomed Jesus' message. It offered them the chance not only to 'enter the kingdom of God' but also to help bring it about. The kingdom, Jesus told them, was for them, however poor, inadequate or guilt-ridden they might be (Luke 6). As proof of this, or rather as a sign (cf. Luke 18) he was healing them 'by the finger of God' (Luke 17.20). God was having compassion on them, through the compassion of Jesus. Their 'sins' were being forgiven (Mark 2.20). In a sense God's reign was already at work. And yet, Jesus insisted, it was their faith which saved them. They were not helpless and hopeless. They had it within their power, oppressed and sick though they may be, to change their miserable situation because they could always put their trust in the hidden power of God and live out their lives on the basis of this trust.

There is no doubt that the success of Jesus' mission was in large part due to the confidence that he was able to instil in the masses of apparently impotent people, both in themselves and more profoundly in God. At the same time his demands on them were very radical indeed, and there were relatively few, it would seem, who were willing to respond to them. Yet Jesus relied wholly on the response of his fellow Jews as a basis for his hope. If they would not respond the kingdom would simply not come. Referring once to the inevitable confrontation with Rome, he mourned the chance which his people had let by:

> And when he drew near and saw the city [Jerusalem] he wept over it, saying, 'Would that even today you knew the things that make for peace! But now they are hid from your eyes. For the days shall come upon you, when your enemies will cast up a bank about you and surround you, and hem you in on every side, and dash you to the ground, you and your children within you, and they will not leave one stone upon another in you; *because you did not know the time of your visitation*' (Luke 19.41–44).

His teaching therefore spelt out in some detail the implications of the response that would make the kingdom possible. His followers were to seek their security and identity in God alone, renouncing the false securities and identities of this world. They were to seek their treasure in heaven, not to 'lay up treasures on earth', because 'where your treasure is there will your heart be also' (Luke 12.33f.). The rich among them were to sell all they had and give it to the poor (Mark 10.17–22) because those who were attached to riches could not enter the kingdom of God (Luke 6.20). 'You cannot serve God and Mammon.' Even attachment to family and nation could be an obstacle (Luke 14.26). Everyone was to be accepted and valued, irrespective of their class or group identity. Enemies, such as the Romans, were to be loved (Luke 6.35). Those who would follow Jesus must, in other words, choose between two ways of life, one based on faith – in oneself, in other humans and in God – and one based on fear, which turns people to money and privilege for protection.

If this was too demanding for most people, it turned out to be virtually impossible for the rich and powerful. Their opposition to Jesus forestalled his hopes, leaving him with only two options: to abandon his mission altogether or to confront the authorities in Jerusalem who were intent on removing him. He was of course removed, and in a publically demonstrative manner. His death served a warning to most Jews that they had better abandon their hopes of this subversive leader or expect a similar fate themselves. For some, however, his death became a symbol of just these hopes, for in that acceptance of death he had given the strongest and most moving witness to this faith in God's kingdom. If the historical opportunity had been lost, there was at least this lasting embodiment of the kingdom in the life and death of this remarkable man.

But how is Jesus relevant to our situation?

It would be methodologically correct at this point to consider the immediate impact of Jesus' life and death on the people of his time, and then move on to the interpretations of Jesus that have been offered in successive generations. But quite apart from the complexity of that intellectual exercise, I think we have an occasion for relating Jesus quite directly to our present situation, which in a number of respects recapitulates his own. We too face an imminent catastrophe of our own making, which is admittedly less tangible, more generalized than that feared by Jesus, but which is also more profoundly threatening since it spells the end, not of the relatively small world of ancient Israel, but of the whole of human life on earth, and possibly of all life on earth. If the catastrophe comes in full, there will be no chance of recovery, no remnant to carry through our human hopes and dreams and possibly redeem the evil we will have brought upon the world. This may well be our last chance. Yet the severity of this threat seems only to enhance the significance of Jesus who had the courage to recognize in the threat of his time a unique historical opportunity for change. Here we must rescue Jesus from the hands of optimists and idealists who see in him only a reflection of their own bland expectations. Jesus really did expect the worst, if his people didn't fundamentally change their way of life. (His expectation was of course born out by events. The inevitable confrontation with Rome came about and the state of Israel was destroyed. The Temple was literally demolished in AD 70 and the Jewish establishment banished in AD 135.) But it was precisely the possibility of the worst that made him believe in a new possibility of the best. One gift he makes to our generation is a special sort of hope, which can see a new world in the ruins of the old.

The fact that his expectation was not fulfilled – there are few scholars who would now dare to suggest that the emergence of the church was precisely what Jesus had in mind – does not, however, invalidate his vision. His own response to the failure of his cause carried it to a deeper level, leaving us with a challenge that surpasses the world of his time. The possibility of the kingdom as a historical reality might have come and gone, at least for a time, but in another, more personal sense the kingdom had come to stay. It had been realized in the life and death of Jesus in such a way that it became open for anyone at any time to enter into it. That is to say, it became possible as a way of life, as an anticipation of a world that was still awaited. This has usually been interpreted as a reduction of the kingdom to an individual ethic, but this I think is a rather serious distortion of it. Although the way of life which Jesus taught and lived was undertaken as an individual choice, the manner of that life was decidedly social. It involved renunciation of the world in so far as the world brought suffering and humiliation to others, but it also involved an active resistance to it, even to the point of dying, and an active attempt to create a new community. In our situation it would surely not be possible to follow Jesus without working to create a social order that treated people fairly and an economic order that could be sustained in future generations, without, therefore, using up resources that could not be renewed. This point should be fairly obvious once we have made the connection between a commitment to the people of the earth and an awareness of the suffering incurred by our modern industrial way of life. But the more important point emerging from Jesus' life is that our salvation does not in the end depend on the success of our mission. Even if in the end we fail to rebuild the world, fail to avert catastrophe, our lives will not have been lived in vain. This is the deeper commitment to which Jesus' life invites us: that we let go anxiety for ourselves, stop worrying about the future and our material security, and give ourselves wholly and unreservedly to God's creation. 'Seek first his kingdom and his justice and all these [material] things will be yours as well' (Matt. 6.33).

We cannot escape a certain paradox in this teaching, because Jesus is telling people to let go the anxiety which made them take him seriously in the first place. Our own quest in this book began with the recognition of global worries, echoing the worries of Jesus and his contemporaries for the future of their country. But his last word to us seems to be, 'Do not be anxious about tomorrow, for tomorrow will be anxious for itself. Let the day's own trouble be sufficient for the day' (Matt. 6.34). The worrying has done its work, though. It has disturbed our prejudices, shaken our illusions. Out of it comes an insight into truth, that is, our (profound) identity with all things in God. Out of that again comes compassion for those who suffer, a will to care and take responsibility. And out of the caring, and receiving of care, there comes a liberating experience of being one with God's creation. In such an experience, provided we trust it, there cannot be room for too much worry.

We do still worry, and so long as we are not perfected in compassion it is just as well that we do. We are involved in a struggle all the time to retain the trust when confronted with threats and disappointments, and to recover it when we have been deceived or overwhelmed. But to reflect on this all too human struggle is only to discover again that the kingdom of God, which we most deeply desire but which always seems to elude us, is always in fact present as an option.

Individuals and collectivities

But this deeper exploration of Jesus' message rather sharpens an issue that came up in conjunction with East/West relations. The scale of the problems we have been looking at makes it difficult to see how any individual commitment could even begin to resolve them. Many people who are aware of these global problems experience a sense of futility in not being able to make a difference or to contribute in any way to the large-scale changes that are called for. In some cases this may be due to contingencies that limit their capacity or opportunity to act: they lack the time or energy or influence. But for all of us there is a general reason to feel ineffectual. It has to do with the fact that the global forces at work have a momentum and power that are beyond any of us to resist. To be more specific, the field of force that has come into view from a global perspective is on too large a scale to include individuals as such. From this height they are not even visible, we could say. The centres of power are located in corporations and governments, not in popular movements or individual action. The system reaches its tentacles into every corner of public and private life so that even the more wealthy or influential among us are determined and perhaps oppressed by it.

There are a number of issues here, and it may be helpful to try and untangle them. There is the question of whether those institutions which claim to have the power really do have it – it may be too much in their interest for us to believe this of them, and not seriously to doubt it. Governments especially want us to believe in their power so that we will readily confirm it at the next election. Also the macro-view misleads us into believing in collective subjects as independent powers in their own right, like mythical giants. While we must face up honestly to the fact that collectivities do behave differently from individuals, and mostly less responsibly,[6] and that their power obviously exceeds the power of individuals greatly, we must not conclude from this that they behave as gigantic, all-powerful gods. They do what they do by the consent and collusion of the individuals who make them up and whose interests they serve, and without that they can surely do nothing. Finally, the daunting thought that the new industrial system enters into every aspect of our lives, making us apparently helpless to resist – I am thinking especially of the insidious power of advertising and television – can just as easily be turned around and made into the reassuring thought that because the system depends on our consent and collaboration, and those of other consumers and users, we do in fact have the power to resist it. The further it reaches into our lives the more we are able to do something about it.

We have noted already (in chapter 2) how the global finance system depends as much on the confidence of share-holders and borrowers as on the availability of hard cash. We see something similar in industrial society at large: its success in maintaining growth and security depends on the faith of masses of people that it can indeed provide these things. It may take only the brave witness of relatively few people to call in question the validity of the whole enterprise. The major collectivities in the world today are based on the quasi-religion of modernity, which is now proving to be somewhat empty. This is a unique opportunity to bear witness to an alternative.

This is not to say that we can ever expect collectivities, however reformed, to show the same moral concern that we expect of individuals. The difference will remain because, as Reinhold Niebuhr argued so forcefully, the interests which hold a collectivity together do not allow it to serve the interests of other groups as well. A nation e.g. is held together by the needs of its members for economic and military security. It is based on a common interest, and to pursue this interest it must struggle against other nations which are similarly motivated by their common interest. It cannot therefore put the interests of another nation first, in an altruistic fashion, without dissolving its own basis. Nations are inevitably competitive and 'selfish'. Similarly, banks and transnational companies give priority to the financial interests of their shareholders. NATO and the Warsaw Pact are constituted for one simple purpose, to provide an adequate defence strategy for the alliance con-cerned. However, we don't have to conclude that bodies such as these are entirely resistant to moral persuasion, especially if we believe that morals arise, at least partly, from an awareness of our mutual interdependence as human beings. All of us take account of others in order to serve our own interests. If we recognize that our interest lies in the give and take of a community we will want to be generous to others and even at times sacrifice our immediate self-interest for the sake of others. We call this enlightened self-interest. The

same logic now applies, in a modified way, to the larger
collectivities which are having to come to terms with the new
interdependence of peoples on a global scale. Their policy of
serving the specific interests of one specific group, at the
possible expense of other interests and other groups, might
have been enlightened in its time, but in the new world
emerging we would have to say that it is not nearly enlightened enough. In this respect the realism of thinkers like
Reinhold Niebuhr is being surpassed by events. What was
idealism at one time – e.g. in the ages of colonialism,
European nationalism or the more recent cold war – has
become realism today. A good example of this is the thawing
of the cold war itself. The old postures of military confrontation are being seen increasingly, even by people in the
military, as counter-productive and possibly suicidal, given
the appalling cost of any actual military engagement between
East and West. In its place there is now talk of 'defensive
defence' and even such nonviolent strategies as confidence
building and economic co-operation. It is a similar logic to
that which guided spiritual visionaries such as Jesus and
Gandhi to look for security in the building of communities of
love and respect. We may not expect collectivities to go that
far but, given the new exigencies of our collective situation,
we can hope that they will go a very long way in that
direction.

Epilogue as dialogue

The main issues of this book have revolved around a confrontation between the profound doubt that arises from the
global crisis and a religious faith that struggles to survive in
the face of it. Let me express this confrontation in the form
of a dialogue between a modern doubter and a Christian
believer who has had to rethink his or her faith quite
radically. The dialogue will certainly represent my own
struggle for understanding in this, which means that I
identify with both sides of the argument, but I think it also
expresses a conflict that many people experience who try to
think theologically, whether they are confessed believers or
not, whether they are Christians or not. The argument will
move from the more obvious challenge to Christian hope

down to the deeper challenges to faith that require deeper responses.

Modern doubter: I speak as a modern person, steeped in modernity and yet fully aware of its weaknesses and inevitable contradictions. In fact I can see little future for the world with its present pursuit of modernity, nor can I see any development without it. What worries me about you believers is that you seem incapable of accepting the inevitabilities of global catastrophe. You seem to think that God or good human sense will save us from these disasters, even though all the evidence points in one direction only, towards the certain destruction of the earth, either in the bang of a nuclear holocaust or in the whimper of ecological decline. The global crisis is not a local, manageable affair; it is a total breakdown of civilized life which can only lead to a global death. To think otherwise is to indulge in idealist illusions.

Radical believer: You say the future is inevitable. That is just as dogmatic as those religious believers who imagine that God has planned the whole of human history from the beginning and invites us simply to accept this plan in faith. The important truth I derive from our religious tradition is that the future is never inevitable. The main thrust of the prophetic tradition is that the future is placed in our hands, to be realized in a covenant relationship with God. This is not to say it is put entirely within our power, since we cannot realize the promised kingdom of God with our power alone. The choice before us is precisely the option between God and the false alternatives we can so easily set up in God's place, viz, the idols. 'Choose you this day whom you will serve', as Joshua said (Joshua 24.15). 'No man can serve two masters', as Jesus said in the Gospels. And from that point of view the relentless movement of modernity has become a new form of idolatry. If we continue in blind loyalty to the idols of modernity, of course we will eventually and inevitably be destroyed. But that is the choice we have to make. We always have the option to choose differently.

Doubter: There are options, I will concede, but modernity is not one of them. We are involved here with a collective development that far exceeds the power of individuals to control. Even politicians and powerful individuals are helpless in this regard. They have choices about what kind of modernization their countries might go for, but they have no choices about whether to pursue modernity. To opt out of the global civilization with its built-in pressures of economic and industrial growth would be to take a road to collective suicide. No country or large company could consciously accept that. Individuals can of course protest and prophesy against this development if they so wish, but it will not make a blind bit of difference. They are only fooling themselves if they think they can. In any case, the idea that they could must surely involve a self-contradiction. If we are free to save our world from destruction through faith in God, we are equally free to destroy it. And if we are free to destroy it, then the God we are supposed to believe in cannot save it. What kind of a God are we left with then? What kind of a God is it who can let his creation be reduced to ashes without being able – or is it willing? – to redeem it?

Believer: It now appears that modernity has become God! The new Zeus or Jupiter that rules our fate. It was just this idea of a fate overruling human lives, indifferent to their needs and resolves, that the early Christians so vigorously rejected. Your God of Fate is no more substantial than that of the Greeks and Romans, even when it appears in modern dress. This powerful shaper of our identity – I don't deny it is powerful – has drawn its power from us, and depends entirely for its strength on our own willing collusion. That means that we are always free *not* to collude, and that resistance, as a public refusal to co-operate, has an immense power of its own out of all proportion to the force at its disposal. More positively, we Christians – and I think many other believers would want to say the same thing – can speak about the creative power of love, even suffering love. It is part of our faith that love makes a difference, despite all appearances to the contrary, while on the other hand the pretentious assertions of human power will prove in the end – in the long run of history – to have achieved very little. As always, the idols will be revealed to have feet of clay.

Doubter: I am touched by your faith. You really do believe that a spiritual awareness can change people's lives. But even if that is so, can we honestly expect a witness of faith to change the course of history? That is to ask for very much more, more than we have a right to expect in view of what we know about human nature. To back a loser is one thing, but to bank on him winning is quite another. But perhaps the thought of failure is too much to bear, especially when we're contemplating the fate of the human race. I would say that what we need most in this situation is the courage, the stoic courage if you like, to accept the essentially tragic character of human life, but also to affirm the good things of life which are actually available to us. To fly in the face of reality with the dream of a utopian future is to turn faith into wishful thinking. As such, I must say, it is a dangerous distraction.

Believer: One thing I do know about human nature is that human beings have a will to live, unless every chance of survival has been taken away from them. When faced with a threat to their lives they will fight, if necessary they will change the way they live. All they need to do this is an understanding of the threat and of the possible ways to avoid it. In the present situation I am really expecting nothing more of them. Once they understand that the world is in danger, and why, they will change. That is simple realism. Of course it is possible that they won't understand, or even choose not to, and therefore not take appropriate action. That is the risk. But then real faith, as I understand it, has always included risk. There are believers, of a kind, who *do* expect a certain, inevitable outcome, guaranteed by God. But that, in my view, is an immature faith which, as you say, turns into wishful thinking. Real faith takes responsibility. It also faces the possibility of failure, but without despair. Tragedy for us is not the last word. We find meaning and hope in knowing what is possible for us humans and our earth and devoting ourselves to it, whatever the outcome.

NOTES

One · Introduction

1. J. M. Roberts, *The Triumph of the West*, BBC Publications 1985.
2. Arnold Toynbee, *The World and the West*, OUP 1953, p. 82.
3. Cf. R. Hooykaas, *Religion and the Rise of Modern Science*, Scottish Academic Press 1972.
4. Cf. E. J. Dijksterhuis, *The Mechanization of the World Picture*, Princeton University Press 1986 (OUP 1961); Fritjof Capra, *The Turning Point*, Bantam Books 1983.
5. Johan Galtung, 'On the last 2,500 years in Western history and some remarks on the coming 500', in Peter Burke (ed.), *The New Cambridge Modern History, vol. XIII; Companion Volume*, CUP 1979, pp. 319, 341.
6. Johan Galtung, art. cit., p. 342.
7. Ibid.
8. I am thinking here of the classic studies by Max Weber, *The Protestant Ethic and the Spirit of Capitalism* (ET: George Allen and Unwin 1930), and by R. H. Tawney, *Religion and the Rise of Capitalism* (Penguin 1938, originally 1926).
9. Tissa Balasuriya, *Planetary Theology*, SCM Press, London and Orbis Books, Maryknoll, 1984, p. 121. I owe my own first inkling of this to a lecture by Fr Balasuriya in 1981. However, it will be seen that my approach is somewhat different from his. He speaks, obviously, from the viewpoint of the South, whereas my view is from the North and the West. More importantly, he focusses his case – the book is rather like a prosecution – on the injustice of the global economic system and on the consequent need for a concerted struggle for justice. I focus more on what I take to be the theological issues underlying the global crisis, but also widen the view to include security and ecological concerns. I don't think the two approaches are incompatible, however.
10. Ibid; cf. p. 122 for a quotation from a relevant Papal Bull of 1452, *Dum diversas*, granting to the king of Portugal 'In the name of our apostolic authority ... the full and entire faculty of invading, conquering, expelling, and reigning over all the kingdoms, the duchies ... of all Saracens, of pagans, and of all infidels, wherever they may be found; of reducing their inhabitants to perpetual slavery, of appropriating to

yourself these kingdoms and all their possessions, for your own use and that of your successors'.

Two · North/South

1. Cf. E. F. Schumacher, *Small is Beautiful: a study of economics as if people mattered*, Blond and Briggs 1973.

2. See H. Lever and C. Huhne, *Debt and Danger; the World Financial Crisis*, Penguin 1985, chs 5–9; Vella Pillay, 'The international economic order and economic crisis', in Diane Elson *et al.*, (eds), *The International Setting*, U204 Third World Studies, 4A–C, The Open University Press, pp. 13–27; Susan George, *A Fate Worse than Debt*, Penguin 1988.

3. David Lomax, *The Debt Crisis*, BBC programme, 20 September 1986.

4. Cf. H. Lever and C. Huhne, *Debt and Danger*, p. 11: 'Since the debt crisis which broke in 1982, those flows have been reversed for each important group of countries in the Third World. International Monetary Fund (IMF) estimates imply that in 1985 there is to be a resource flow from the seven largest Third World borrowers to their more prosperous creditors worth $32 billion, or nearly one-fifth of their entire earnings from the sales of their exports of goods and services.' More recent reports from Oxfam confirm that this was in fact the case and that in subsequent years the situation has not improved: see e.g. John Clark's report *For Richer for Poorer*, Oxfam 1986.

5. Alan Garcia, 'A debt stranglehold that must be broken', *The Guardian*, 19 December 1986.

6. The Brandt Commission, *Common Crisis*, Pan 1983, p. 18.

7. William Clark, *Cataclysm; the North-South Conflict of 1987*, Sidgwick and Jackson 1984; Sphere Books 1985.

8. This is confirmed by H. Lever and C. Huhne, *Debt and Danger*, p. 12: the banks' 'outstanding lending to the Third World outstrips their own capital by a factor of two or more'.

9. Cf. Lever and Huhne, op. cit., p. 12: 'The world's financial safety ...'; and p. 122: 'The influence of a serious default ... devastating effects'.

10. William Clark, *Cataclysm*, Sphere edition, pp. 125f.

11. Cf. the Brandt Commission follow-up report, *Common Crisis*, pp. 4f.

12. This belief was reaffirmed very strongly in the Brandt Report, *North-South*, Pan 1980, e.g. p. 64: 'This principle of mutuality of interest has been at the centre of our discussion'; and p. 269: 'The self-interest of nations can now only be effectively pursued through taking account of mutual interests'; but the mutuality in question was clearly that of the modern, free-market economy.

13. Cf. Eric Hobsbawm, *Industry and Empire*, Penguin 1969.

14. I have developed this idea from the sociologist Thomas Luckmann, *The Invisible Religion*, Macmillan 1967, and the theologian Paul Tillich, *Christianity and the Encounter of World Religions*, Columbia University Press 1963, ch. 1. On the implicit religiosity of modern commercial life I have been struck by the insights of C. Wright Mills, *The White Collar*, OUP 1951, especially the section on 'the biggest bazaar in the world', pp. 166ff.

Three · East/West

1. James O'Connell, 'Political structures and process in the contemporary world', paper to the Dayschool on the Theology of Peace, University of Birmingham, 22 May 1988, p. 10.

2. Cf. Lynne Atwood and Derek Jones, *The Cold War Game*, Channel Four Broadcasting Support Services 1988; Fred Halliday, *The Making of the Second Cold War*, Verso, London 1983; Noam Chomsky, Jonathan Steele, John Gittings, *Superpowers in Collision: the Cold War Now*, revd edn, Penguin 1984.

3. Cf. Stephen Shenfield, *The Nuclear Predicament: explorations in Soviet ideology*, Routledge and Kegan Paul 1987.

4. Cf. the figures in Jim Garrison and Pyare Shivpuri, *The Russian Threat: its myths and realities*, Gateway Books, London 1983, p. 164: 'The NATO Alliance has been consistently outspending the USSR and its Eastern European allies over the past twenty-five years. This is the conclusion of the US Arms Control and Disarmament Agency which points out that between 1970 and 1979 NATO outspent the WTO by over \$200 billion, \$1,946.6 billion against \$1,739.6 billion.' On the relation of defence expenditure to national budgets throughout the world see *The Stockholm International Peace Research Institute (SIPRI) Handbook*, 1985.

5. 'Exterminism' is a term used by E. P. Thompson to describe the logic of the arms race as tending towards mass destruction. I am using the phrase 'subjective exterminism' to describe a widespread human attitude which embraces this process fatalistically, or with apocalyptic élan. Cf. Thompson's 'Notes on exterminism, the last stage of civilization', *New Left Review* 121, London 1980; his and others' *Exterminism and Cold War*, Verso, London 1982; and Rudolf Bahro, 'Dimensions of exterminism and the idea of general emancipation', in *Building the Green Movement*, GMP Publishers, London 1985, pp. 142–158; and 'Conditions for a socialist perspective in the late twentieth century', in *Socialism and Survival*, Heretic Books 1982, pp. 124ff.

6. Jeremy Holmes, 'The psychology of nuclear disarmament', in Ian Fenton (ed.), *The Psychology of Nuclear Conflict*, Coventure, London 1986, p. 73.

7. On the Soviet perception of these speeches see Jonathan Steele, *Limits of Soviet Power*, 2nd edn, Penguin 1985, pp. 255f.

8. Cf. E. P. Thompson, *Beyond the Cold War*, Merlin Press 1982.

9. In the journal *Voprosy Filosofi*: quoted by Martin Walker, 'Is anyone listening?', *The Guardian*, 18 February 1987, p. 27.

10. Quoted in Martin Walker, art. cit.

11. Dorothy Rowe has written about the psychological problems in confronting the situation in *Living with the Bomb*, Routledge and Kegan Paul, 1985; as has Joanne Macy, *Despair and Personal Power in the Nuclear Age*, New Society Publishers, Philadelphia 1983.

12. Cf. Jonathan Schell, *The Fate of the Earth*, Picador 1982, esp. p. 8.

13. This is the title of the report from the Palme Commission on Disarmament and Security Issues, modelled on the report of the Brandt Commission. It concluded that it was 'of paramount importance to replace the doctrine of mutual deterrence. Our alternative is common security. There can be no hope of victory in a nuclear war, the two sides would be united in suffering and destruction. They can survive only together. They must achieve security not against the adversary but together with him. International security must rest on a commitment to joint survival rather than on a threat of mutual destruction' – Olaf Palme's introduction to the Independent Commission on Disarmament and Security Issues, *Common Security*, Pan 1982, p. ix.

14. I wouldn't say, though, as Jim Garrison does, that 'God slipped us the bomb' (*The Darkness of God*, SCM Press, London and Eerdmans, Grand Rapids 1982, p. 211), since this resolves our dilemma too easily, suggesting that it is after all God's responsibility and not ours. I prefer Gordon Kaufman's reasoning on this point, (*Theology for a Nuclear Age*, Manchester University Press 1985) although with him I am left wondering what it now means to trust in God. Between them Garrison and Kaufman pose a serious theological problem, reminiscent of the debate in the fifth century between Augustine and Pelagius on predestination and free will.

15. Jim Garrison's treatment of apocalyptic in relation to present day attitudes (*The Darkness of God*, pp. 95–97 especially) is very illuminating. See also the lively discussion of modern apocalytic and associated problems in the symposium, Alan Race (ed.), *Theology against the Nuclear Horizon*, SCM Press 1988.

16. I take this view of the inevitable self-interest of collectivities from the impressive writings of Reinhold Niebuhr on this theme, notably his *Moral Man and Immoral Society* of 1932 (Scribners, New York and SCM Press, London 1963). I pick up the issue for a fuller discussion in the Conclusion.

Four · People/Planet

1. Cf. Ann and Paul Ehrlich, *Earth*, Thames and Hudson 1987, pp. 109–130.

2. Cf. Norman Myers (ed.), *The Gaia Atlas of Planet Management*, Pan 1985, pp. 40–42.

3. Cf. Norman Myers (ed.), p. 154.

4. World Commission on Environment and Development (ed. Gro Harlem Bruntland *et al.*), *Our Common Future*, OUP 1987.

5. This is one of the main conclusions of the penetrating analysis by Barry Commoner, *The Closing Circle: confronting the environmental crisis*, Jonathan Cape 1972.

6. Even in Plato's day there were instances of massive soil erosion as a result of the over-cultivation of the land. He wrote, 'What now remains compared with what existed is like the skeleton of a sick man, all the fat and soft earth having been washed away, and only the bare framework of the land being left.' The main difference today is the scale of the problem.

7. *Our Common Future*, p. 343.

8. Cf. Norman Myers' epilogue to his (ed.) *Gaia Atlas of Planet Management*, Pan 1985, p. 258, e.g.: 'As for our knowledge of the effects of human action, very few nations establish the true rates of soil loss, deforestation, or pollution; some cannot accurately count their hungry, poverty-stricken or workless populations. In the oceans, we do not know the size of our fish stocks we are depleting, nor the rate of the spread of the toxins we pour out. Our ignorance is so vast, in fact, that we are not aware of it.'

9. Barbara Ward and René Dubos, *Only One Earth*, an unofficial report commissioned for the United Nations Conference on the Human Environment, Penguin 1972, p. 173.

10. Commoner, *The Closing Circle: confronting the environmental crisis*, p. 119.

11. *Our Common Future*, p. 101; Myers, *The Gaia Atlas of Planet Management*, p. 108.

12. *Our Common Future*, pp. 206–208.

13. Myers, *The Gaia Atlas of Planet Management*, pp. 202ff.

14. Edward Goldsmith *et al.*, *A Blueprint for Survival*, Tom Stacey 1972, pp. 14f.

15. Cf. S. N. Eisenstadt's Introduction to his (ed.), *Patterns of Modernity*, Francis Pinter 1987.

16. Cf. Commoner, *The Closing Circle: confronting the environmental crisis*, pp. 39f.

17. Ibid., pp. 12, 32.

18. E.g. Fritjof Capra, *The Turning Point: science, society and the rising culture*, Bantam Books 1983.

19. Martin Buber, *I and Thou*, trans. Walter Kaufmann, T. & T. Clark 1970 (original German edition 1923), pp. 57f.
20. William James, *The Will to Believe*, Longmans Green 1937, p. 86.
21. Dorothée Sölle and Shirley A. Cloyes, *To Work and to Love: A Theology of Creation*, Fortress Press, Philadelphia 1984, p. 11.
22. Cf. H. Paul Santmire, *The Travail of Nature: the ambiguous ecological promise of Christian theology*, Fortress Press, Philadelphia 1985, pp. 202ff on Paul's apocalyptic theology; also J. Christiaan Beker, *Paul the Apostle: the triumph of God in life and thought*, Fortress Press, Philadelphia 1980.
23. Celano, *Vita Prima*, 80; quoted in Santmire, pp. 115f.
24. *Our Common Future*, p. 343; fuller text quoted above. R. J. Berry regards it as the key to 'environmental ethics' that we are 'both *apart from* nature and *part of* nature': *The Conservation and Development Programme for the UK: a response to the World Conservation Strategy*, ed. the Programme Organizing Committee, Kogan Page 1983, p. 412.
25. This gives new meaning to Dietrich Bonhoeffer's important account of the human situation around the statement, derived from the philosopher Kant, that 'man has come of age': *Letters and Papers from Prison*, SCM Press, London and Macmillan, New York 1953 and subsequent editions.

Five · Conclusion

1. This was Paul Tillich's preferred definition; cf. e.g. his *Systematic Theology*, vol. I (Chicago University Press 1951; Nisbet 1953; SCM Press 1978.), p. 16: 'Idolatry is the elevation of a preliminary concern to ultimacy ... Something essentially finite is given infinite significance (the best example is the contemporary idolatry of religious nationalism). The conflict between the finite basis of such a concern and its infinite claim leads to a conflict of ultimates; it radically contradicts the biblical commandments ...'
2. Cf. Joanne Macy, *Despair and Personal Power in the Nuclear Age*, New Society Publishers, Philadelphia 1983.
3. The visionary thought of Pierre Teilhard de Chardin may be helpful here, in that he envisages the human task of integration on the pattern of evolutionary changes in the past, and one that will raise evolution itself to a new level. See e.g. his *Phenomenon of Man*, Collins, London and Harper and Row, New York 1959 (original French edition 1955). It should be said though that his use of evolutionary theory is rather speculative.
4. I can however mention the titles of some important recent works: J. D. M. Derrett, *Jesus' Audience: the social and psychological environment in which he worked*, Darton, Longman and Todd 1972; Albert Nolan, *Jesus before Christianity*, Darton Longman and Todd 1977 and Orbis Books,

Maryknoll 1978; E. P. Sanders, *Jesus and Judaism*, SCM Press London and Fortress Press, Philadelphia 1985; Geza Vermes, *Jesus the Jew*, 2nd edn, SCM Press, London and Fortress Press, Philadelphia, 1983; Geza Vermes, *Jesus and the World of Judaism*, Penguin 1983; Wolfgang Stegemann, *The Gospel of the Poor*, Fortress Press, Philadelphia 1984; Wolfgang Stegemann and Luise Schottrof, *Jesus and the Gospel of the Poor*, Orbis Books, Maryknoll 1986; Norman Gottwald, *The Hebrew Bible*, Fortress Press, Philadelphia 1985; George V. Pixley, *God's Kingdom*, SCM Press, London and Orbis Books, Maryknoll 1981; Gerd Theissen, *The Shadow of the Galilean; the quest of the historical Jesus in narrative form*, SCM Press, London and Fortress Press, Philadelphia 1987.

5. This view is based on research by Lloyd Gaston in *No Stone on Another*, Leiden 1970.

6. This was a point made at the end of chapter 3, with note 16.